FLAG FEN

Life and Death of a Prehistoric Landscape

FLAG FEN

Life and Death of a Prehistoric Landscape

FRANCIS PRYOR

TEMPUS

This book is dedicated to Tim Taylor, Philip Clarke and everyone concerned
with the Channel 4 series *Time Team*, that has done so much to make
archaeology accessible to the public.

First published 2005

Tempus Publishing Limited
The Mill, Brimscombe Port,
Stroud, Gloucestershire, GL5 2QG
www.tempus-publishing.com

British Library Cataloguing in Publication Data.
A catalogue record for this book is available from the British Library.

ISBN 0 7524 2900 0

Typesetting and origination by Tempus Publishing Limited
Printed in Great Britain

Contents

Acknowledgements   6

Preface   7

Introduction: Flag Fen in a nutshell   9

1 The Fens   12

2 Archaeology in the Peterborough area   30

3 The first farmers (4000–2500 BC)   55

4 The earlier Bronze Age (2500–1500 BC)   72

5 The later Bronze Age (1500–700 BC)   99

6 The Iron Age (700 BC–AD 43)   160

Appendix: Planning a visit to Flag Fen   181

Further Reading   183

Glossary   184

Index   186

Acknowledgements

I would like to record my special gratitude to Toby Fox, General Manager at Flag Fen, and to the Trustees of Fenland Archaeological Trust who made it possible for me to spend so much time rewriting this book.

Preface

This book is a major revision of one I wrote for the joint English Heritage/ Batsford Books series, which was published in 1991 (*Flag Fen: Prehistoric Fenland Centre*). In the intervening years there has been a vast amount of new material which has substantially altered the way we now see this remarkable site and its landscape. I have attempted, with the essential help of many distinguished collaborators, to draw this wealth of material together in a detailed academic report: *The Flag Fen Basin: Archaeology and environment of a Fenland landscape*, English Heritage Archaeological Report, published in 2001. In this book I will refer to this report as the Flag Fen Basin Report. It is a matter of great sadness to everyone involved with Flag Fen that David Coombs, author of the large study of the metalwork (chapter 10 of the Flag Fen Basin Report), died of cancer in April 2002. Dave was much loved in archaeology and he will be missed enormously.

When Peter Kemmis Betty (who commissioned the 1991 book) suggested the idea of reworking *Flag Fen: Prehistoric Fenland Centre*, for Tempus, I was at first enthusiastic. I even suggested the new subtitle, which gives this book a slightly different slant to its predecessor. Then, when I realised just how much rewriting was needed, I have to admit that my enthusiasm waned. In fact it very nearly died altogether: *so* many things had changed. I knew I would have to do a very major rewrite. Perhaps the biggest change in our interpretation of the archaeological evidence was the inhabited 'lake village' concept – in which we no longer believe. Rereading the original text it is quite apparent that my ideas had only partly changed. I still clung onto the earlier interpretations, despite the fact that they were manifestly wrong. That of itself is interesting. We sometimes forget how much of ourselves we invest in our ideas, be they never so wrong. So if you already possess the earlier book, may I (cheekily) suggest you also purchase this one, as it will provide an indication of the extent to which archaeological interpretations can alter over a relatively short time.

There were other complications, too, the worst of which was the disastrous fire which took place on my birthday at Flag Fen in January 2000. The flames destroyed most of my slide collection, with the result that many of the illustrations that appeared in the first book can no longer be reproduced. I particularly regret the loss of the early photos I took in the first weeks of investigation, back in November 1982. I found it strange the way that the memories seemed to grow dim, and then vanish, with the loss of the slides. I sometimes think those fading memories provide a parable for the presence of archaeological sites within our national psyche: forget about them and effectively they vanish from our collective consciousness. As I write, the two-minute silence outside reminds me that both effort and ritual are needed, if memories are to persist and not to fade.

Francis Pryor,
Armistice Day, 2004

Introduction:
Flag Fen in a nutshell

I mentioned in my Preface that this is a major rewrite of a book I originally wrote 15 years ago. The trouble is that I have lived with Flag Fen for all of those 15 years; consequently it is easy for me to take my knowledge of the site for granted and to assume that my readers also share that knowledge. Recently, however, I have spent time working away from Flag Fen, writing books and making television films, and in the process I have been able to stand back from the site. So when I started on this rewrite, by reading through what I had originally written, I was struck by the fact that nowhere did I describe the complex archaeology of the Flag Fen basin in a simple, clear way that readers could refer to, when things became muddled or confused. I freely admit that the story of discovery told in the following chapters is not always straightforward. This is because I am keen not to lose the feeling that archaeological research itself is rarely straightforward, despite what some would have us believe. Hence this introductory nutshell.

The area I have named the Flag Fen basin is an embayment of low-lying land situated on the western margins of the Fens, immediately south-east of Peterborough (*1*). To the east and west the land gradually rises and becomes flood-free. The eastern dryland is known as Fengate, and that to the west as Northey (*2*). Fengate lies at the edge of what one might think of as 'mainland' England, whereas Northey is part of a large 'island' in the Fens, which includes the market town of Whittlesey. The Northey peninsula is separated from the rest of Whittlesey 'island' by the modern, canalised, course of the River Nene. Between Fengate and Northey is the low-lying wetland landscape of Flag Fen. Peats began to form here as conditions became wetter, around 2000 BC.

The archaeology of Fengate has been studied in some detail. It begins before 3000 BC with a series of Neolithic shrines and other features, which may have been arranged along an ancient routeway. Sometime around 2500 BC, at the start of the Bronze Age, the earlier landscape was elaborated into one of the first field systems in Britain. The fields were defined by ditches and were laid out roughly at right angles to the developing wetland. They were subdivided into blocks of land that were separated by double-ditched droveways, which ran down to the wetland edge. These fields were intended for the use of livestock. Their farmers

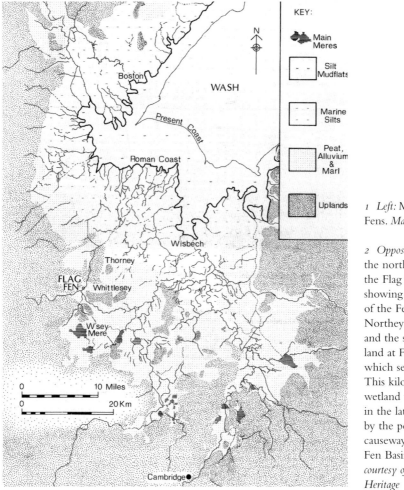

KEY:

- Main Meres
- Silt Mudflats
- Marine Silts
- Peat, Alluvium & Marl
- Uplands

1 Left: Map of the Fens. *Martin Redding*

2 Opposite: Plan of the northern part of the Flag Fen basin, showing the location of the Fengate and Northey field systems and the strait of wetter land at Flag Fen which separates them. This kilometre-wide wetland was traversed in the late Bronze Age by the post alignment causeway. *From the* Flag Fen Basin Report, *courtesy of English Heritage*

lived in small farmsteads dispersed across the landscape. There is now good evidence to suggest that a closely similar landscape of ditched fields also existed across Flag Fen, on the Northey fen-edge.

In the Middle Bronze Age, around 1300 BC, and at a time when the field systems at either side had begun to experience difficulties caused by increasing wetness, a causeway was driven across Flag Fen, from Fengate to Northey. This causeway, known as the post alignment, was constructed of large posts arranged in five rows. These posts helped to secure a build-up of horizontal timbers, which provided the causeway surface. Closer to the Northey side of Flag Fen, and in a particularly low-lying area, the post alignment was enlarged into an artificial platform, also made from timber. The precise purpose of this platform has yet to be fully revealed.

At certain times it seems that the causeway was also used as a ceremonial centre. These ceremonies involved the deposition of probably thousands of metal,

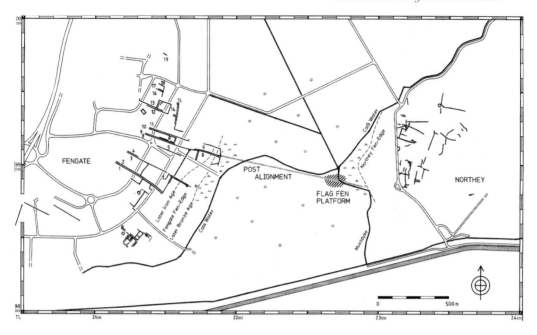

stone, shale, ceramic and other objects, together with cuts of meat, food and other perishable items. These things were placed in the waters of Flag Fen, both within the timbers of the causeway and along its south-western, or 'inland', side.

The last timbers of the post alignment and platform were added shortly after 900 BC, in the Late Bronze Age, but the site of the alignment, which would still have been visible during the drier months of the year, continued to be visited, and offerings were made there, throughout the Iron Age.

The Bronze Age fields at either end of the post alignment began to be abandoned from about 1400 BC, and there was a shift southwards, towards slightly higher ground. By about 700-600 BC the process of abandonment was largely complete. The livestock landscape of the Bronze Age was followed, in the Iron Age, by a landscape dominated by mixed farming of both cereals and livestock. By now the emphasis was shifting towards the drier hinterland, as a single large farm droveway clearly demonstrates. The settlement pattern altered too: from about 600 BC we see the appearance of the first nucleated, village-style settlements that replaced the isolated farmsteads of the Bronze Age.

The transition into Roman times appears to have been smooth and uneventful. Pottery found there shows that the substantial Iron Age farm near the Cat's Water in Fengate continued to be used into the third century AD. Finally, the area has not produced evidence for post-Roman nor Anglo-Saxon settlement, almost certainly because conditions were too wet underfoot. By now it was an area reserved for seasonal pasture – hence the name Fengate, which means 'road to the fen'.

Those then are the bare bones of our story. In the following pages I will try to explain why so simple a tale took over 30 years to unravel.

I

The Fens

Sadly Peterborough is not a city known for the richness of its visitor attractions, especially when compared with York, just a short distance away up the East Coast Main Line. Instead it is perhaps better known as a bustling, modern city of extraordinary vigour. Its diverse legacy of medieval and Romano-British remains is well known, but today it has become almost equally famous for its prehistoric heritage which can find few rivals in eastern England. Nowadays the city owes its success to modern communications: principally those two great arterial routes, the Great North Road (the A1) and the main London to Edinburgh railway line.

In remoter times, however, the region's prosperity depended, to a large part, on the Fens. To outsiders this was a region of mire, marsh gas and disease, but to those who lived in and around the wetter ground it was a place of extraordinary richness and diversity. I will let the splendid words of the twelfth-century chronicler Hugh Candidus set the scene:

> Now Burch [Peterborough] is situated in the region of Gyrwas [the Fens], because the same fen begins there on the eastern side, extending for sixty miles or more. The same is very valuable to men because there are obtained in abundance all things needful for them that dwell thereby, logs and stubble for kindling, hay for the feeding of their beasts, thatch for the roofing of their houses, and many other things of use and profit, and moreover it is very full of fish and fowl. There are divers rivers and many other waters there, and moreover great fishponds. In all these things that district is very rich. So this Burch is built in a fair spot, and a goodly, because on the one side it is rich in fenland, and in goodly waters, with many fertile meads and pastures, and on the other it has abundance of plough lands and woodlands, with many fertile meads and pastures. On all sides it is beautiful to look upon and easy to approach on foot, save only on the eastern side where there is no coming to it save in a boat.

This book is mainly concerned with Hugh's 'eastern side', the land around the eastern fringes of Peterborough. This ground is now covered by roads and factories. In the distant past, however, it was host to a succession of farms, villages and hamlets. Today the district is known as (Peterborough's) Eastern Industry, but until very recently it retained its Norse name of Fengate, or 'road leading to the fen'. About 800m (0.5 miles) east of Fengate, in the peaty landscape that was flooded until very recently, sits the superbly preserved site of Flag Fen in its own self-contained wetland about a 1km wide. Beyond that peat-filled 'strait' was more dry land, known as Northey. Northey was (and is) a short headland or peninsula protruding from the large natural 'island' of Whittlesey which is the second largest 'island' in the Fens – second only to the Isle of Ely. Incidentally, I put the word 'island' in quotes because it was rarely a real island permanently surrounded by water. More usually it would have been a drier area surrounded by acres and acres of marsh and reed bed. Only in the wettest of winters would it have been a true island.

In the following pages I shall attempt to reconstruct life in Fengate and Flag Fen from the beginnings of farming in the Neolithic period (c.4500 BC) until the widespread flooding of the later Roman period (c.AD 300). There must be a tendency, when writing about 30 years' work in the same place, to become over-possessive and to think in terms of the first person singular. I suppose Fengate and Flag Fen have become part of my make-up. But I must emphasise that both sites were in fact team efforts. The teams who dug them were usually quite small – perhaps six to eight people, reaching a maximum in mid-summer of about 14 to 18 in all. Within the evolving teams were key specialists, many of whom still keep in touch with the project, and whose work will be discussed in the appropriate places below. All of that said, the fact remains I, personally, have become deeply involved with the entire landscape. Some might object that this means I am unable to take a disinterested or dispassionate view. And maybe they're right. But I have to say I don't think that matters much, because it's a myth to suppose that any archaeologist can remove him or herself from their work. It's only human to become personally involved and as we're trying to investigate the lives of long-dead humans – and our subject, archaeology, is after all a humanity – I don't think that it's necessarily a bad thing to identify with the object of one's researches. Anyhow, it's something I felt I ought to admit to from the very outset.

It would be impossible to reconstruct patterns of ancient life without also attempting to rebuild an approximation of the ancient landscape too – as people had to live out their lives within a physical environment. When I originally wrote this I believed that the actual shape of the landscape played a large part in the way people structured their lives. Now I realise that the fields, streams, posts, gullies and pits of the landscape were far less important than the mental map people carried in their heads. This map would have been peopled by stories, myths and legends and it would also have been shaped by the deeds, real and imaginary, of the individual's own relatives and ancestors. In short it was a landscape of the mind and it's something I would love to recreate, but sadly I lack the evidence, or perhaps the confidence to do it justice. Mark Edmonds has come as close as anyone in his remarkable book on *Neolithic Ancestral Geographies*. Writing about the Fens, although his words could equally well apply to other prehistoric landscapes, he gives us a glimpse of a vanished world:

> Stories may have been told of the creation of the land and its first occupation, of mythic events and ancestral struggles. These stories may have had a timeless quality, perhaps like the ancestral realm itself, but they could be linked to the present by specific ancestors and long genealogies. Acknowledged in the pattern of daily life, these values and distinctions were brought into focus through rites of passage, oral tradition and the passing on of practical and ritual knowledge.★

THE FEN LANDSCAPE

Given Peterborough's location at the extreme edge of Britain's largest natural wetland, we cannot avoid a discussion of the Fens. Estimates of their size vary, but 400,000ha (1 million acres) is a widely accepted figure. Most of the land lies below the 4m (12.5ft) contour, although higher 'islands' protrude above it in places. Today the Fens occupy significant parts of two counties (Lincolnshire and Cambridgeshire), but they also include smaller areas of Norfolk and Suffolk. If you include the wide river valleys that drain into the Fenland basin, then sizeable areas of Bedfordshire and Northamptonshire are involved too. All in all, it's a large and hugely diverse landscape – or landscapes. Simply to refer to it as 'a wetland' is wholly to miss the point. I very much doubt whether prehistoric Fen folk would have regarded themselves as wetlanders. No, they lived their lives in a richer than average environment, which was sometimes subject to severe flooding. Water was something they knew and understood. It was a part of their everyday existence, just as fells, cliffs and scree-covered slopes were familiar to the people who lived in the uplands. These things were facts of life, but they didn't define or shape the way people responded to their surroundings. That was something that came from within their culture, which in turn had infinitely complex origins, extending back over many millennia, perhaps as far as the last Ice Age, over 10,000 years ago.

The pre-Roman Fen was a country of reeds, willow sedge and wildfowl, of biting winter winds and abundant fish and fowl. Today the land is very different: huge fields of wheat and sugar beet are separated by dead straight dykes with no trees to fill the emptiness around (3). The sky itself is part of this landscape and it blends seamlessly with the ground beneath. No other landscape can demonstrate so clearly why the ancients considered the heavens a vast dome.

★Mark Edmonds, *Ancestral Geographies of the Neolithic: Landscapes, monuments and memory*, p.31 (Routledge, London, 1999)

3 The Fens today: the road runs on a bank alongside the large drainage dyke or river. In the distance is the chimney of a nineteenth-century steam-driven pump, which would have raised water from the surrounding land into the main drain

In a flat, naturally treeless environment the horizon looks like a huge circle and it becomes quite easy to understand why prehistoric communities in Britain attached so much importance to circular monuments, such as henges, round barrows, stone and timber circles. These special places incorporated, tamed and symbolised the natural world in which they stood. Indeed, their shape made them and their creators an integral part of the natural order of things. It was as if human culture had arisen from nature – the hills and trees, sun, moon and stars. It was therefore in harmony with the mythical forces which had once fashioned, and now controlled, all things.

Some still see the Fen landscape as flat and monotonous; Fenmen, traditionally self-contained and somewhat taciturn, are inclined to think differently. The great palaeobotanist Sir Harry Godwin put it succinctly:

> … the flatness provides that feature of a display of the vast hemisphere of sky impossible to match elsewhere in Britain and the key to the affection the landscape generates in the hearts of resident fenmen. As one, unexpectedly communicative, explained to me: 'any fool can appreciate mountain scenery but it takes a man of discernment to appreciate the Fens'.★

★Sir Harry Godwin, *Fenland: Its Ancient Past and Uncertain Future*, p.1 (Cambridge University Press, 1978)

On a winter's evening, with a bitter north-easterly blowing from off the Wash, I must admit I find the process of appreciation greatly aided by a pint of two of Elgood's excellent Wisbech Ales. The region also produces some of the finest sausages money can buy, being positioned directly between the two fine, long-established, butchery traditions of Norfolk and Lincolnshire.

One feature of a near-level landscape is, however, often overlooked. In flat country the smallest prominences can acquire a very special significance. During a wet season a rise in the land of just a few centimetres can make the difference between life and death. It is not for nothing that Fen folk have always had a keen eye for topography.

We will see shortly how the Fens were 'tamed' from being a watery landscape to one in which the arable farmer now reigns supreme, and there can be little doubt that this 'taming' process has rid Fenland of much of its mystery and romance. Nevertheless the region has a distinctive feel all of its own. It takes someone who knows the Fens, and who has lived and worked there, to write about them properly. Dorothy Sayers is such a person: she captures the essence of the place with absolute topographical precision. This is illustrated by her description, from *The Nine Tailors*, of Bunter driving Lord Peter Wimsey across the deep Fen to the higher 'Marshland' country around Wisbech ('Walbeach': like all her names, authentic-sounding but non-existent). Incidentally, the book is set between the wars, hence the reference to pumping windmills which have almost all, sadly, vanished:

> Mile after mile the flat road reeled behind them. Here a windmill, there a solitary farmhouse, there a row of poplars strung along the edge of a reed-grown dyke. Wheat, potatoes, beet, mustard and wheat again ... . A long village street with a grey and ancient church tower, a red-brick chapel, and the vicarage set in a little oasis of elm and horse-chestnut, and then once more dyke and windmill, wheat, mustard and grassland. And as they went, the land flattened more and more, if a flatter flatness were possible, and the windmills became more numerous, and on the right hand the silver streak of the Wale River came back into view, broader now, swollen with the water of the Thirty-foot and of Harper's Cut and St Simon's Eau, and winding and spreading here and there, with a remembrance of its ancient leisure. Then, ahead of the great circle of the horizon, a little bunch of spires and roofs and a tall tree or so, and beyond them the thin masts of shipping. And so, by bridge and bridge the travellers came to Walbeach, once a great port, but stranded now far inland with the silting of the marshes and the choking of the Wale outfall ... .

However, before we become wholly swamped in mist and mystery, we should consider how and when the Fens formed. It used to be thought that certain deposits which looked very similar over large areas of the Fens – the most famous of these being the so-called Buttery or Fen Clay – were laid down at the same time. So the sequence was seen as being relatively straightforward with a Lower Peat separated from an Upper Peat by the Fen Clay which formed during much wetter conditions in the later Neolithic and earlier Bronze Age. But sadly it was not as simple as that. A major study of the ancient environments in Fenland was carried out by Martyn Waller for English Heritage's Fenland Survey.★ This was published in 1994 and it established beyond doubt that the simple scheme of earlier times just didn't work, largely because the two peats and the intervening Fen Clays didn't form at the same time right across the Fens. Instead, Waller and his colleagues showed that the ancient Fens were a very diverse, heterogeneous place, with numerous, often self-contained smaller environments, each of which had their own history of development. Sometimes it was possible to link them together, but by no means always. The Flag Fen basin was just such an environment. It was a gently shelving, flat bay or embayment just south of Peterborough and the lower-lying areas started to become waterlogged sometime around 2000 BC. But why were conditions getting wetter? What motivated these environmental changes?

The principle is simple: about 10,000 years ago, at the end of the last Ice Age, the climate grew milder and meltwater from the Ice Age ice fields flowed into the world's oceans, causing global sea levels to rise. It was a process that was exacerbated by the fact that warmer water expands in volume – which is why the current rise in sea level will take so very long to slow down. The first areas to feel the effects of these changes were low-lying, and the North European plain, now occupied by the North Sea, was one such area. River valleys flooded first and were enlarged into bays, such as the Wash. The Fens are a large natural depression, inland of the Wash, that was not quite deep enough to be permanently inundated by the North Sea. Instead, the area began to get wet in its lowest-lying river valleys around 7000 BC, at which point peats started to form. Thereafter the area was flooded by the sea during storm tides, or by rivers bursting their natural banks when in spate. These processes were under way very approximately between 5000 and 3000 BC, depending on how low-lying the land was. Peterborough sits on the western or inland edge of the Fens and is relatively high by Fenland standards; its fens therefore flooded quite late (as we have seen, around 2000 BC).

What were the general effects of these flooding processes? The first thing to emphasise is that they were complex, and even after Waller's remarkable efforts they still require much unravelling; what follows is a simplified version of the true story.

We could do worse than borrow Dorothy Sayers' literary device and make an imaginary journey across the varied soils of Fenland, starting at Wisbech, near the Wash, and heading inland, towards Peterborough, which was where the dryland of 'mainland' Britain begins. The so-called 'Marshland' countryside around Wisbech

---

★M. Waller, *The Fenland Project, No. 9: Flandrian environmental change in Fenland*, East Anglian Archaeology, 70 (1994)

(and the silty soils near the Wash) are the only parts of Fenland that somehow feel old: there are trees and hedges, lanes meander and massive medieval churches dominate the dispersed hamlets; as such it can hardly be considered as typical of Fenland at all. The silt soils are all of marine origin and are extraordinarily productive for the farmer. This is where most of our vegetables are grown. However, the Marshland landscape need not detain the prehistorian long, as the silts that form it were mainly laid down by marine floods in the later Iron Age; consequently prehistoric (i.e. pre-Roman) finds are very rare indeed.

West of Marshland we move into a more open landscape of heavier clay and silt soils. These large, open fields are traversed by raised banks of silt known locally as 'roddons' or 'rodhams'. The roddons wander across the landscape in a seemingly aimless fashion, but when viewed from the air they can be seen to form elaborate, tree-like, branching patterns. Their precise interpretation is still a matter for some debate, but they are undoubtedly the remains of marine water courses, and most probably tidal creeks, dating from a time when the North Sea covered large parts of south Lincolnshire and Cambridgeshire. When the creeks were active they flowed through a landscape of peats and peaty clays. The water they contained carried a heavy load of suspended silts; but when the tide turned, the water briefly stopped moving and dumped part of its suspended load on the creek bed.

Over the years the material built up and sometimes the creek actually blocked up and new courses were formed. Occasionally the remains of the last stream channel are still visible, usually showing up as a thin, dark line on an aerial photo. The dark mark of the last course, wending its way down the centre of the creek forms a striking contrast with the white silts of the rest of the roddon. After drainage, the lighter soils through which the creek had cut its course would tend to shrink as the peats and finer-grained organic matter (such as clays) dried out, leaving the heavier material (usually coarser-grained silts) in the creek beds to project *above* the ground surface they had once flowed through. In other words the original topography of the landscape had been turned upsidedown. The reversal of the landscape's original contours – where what was once high is now low, and vice versa – often makes the reconstruction and interpretation of prehistoric Fenland landscapes very difficult indeed.

The soils of Marshland essentially derived from the North Sea, but the Fen country immediately inland, to the south and west, is far more complex: the material filling the roddons is plainly marine, but the courses themselves were cut by rivers and streams making their way towards the sea. Material forming the land around the roddons can derive from a number of sources: earlier spreads of sea-borne silts, river-borne (alluvial) clays or peats – some formed locally, others washed in from elsewhere. In places, for example east of the old 'island' at Thorney, there is evidence for substantial marine inundations (or transgressions) in the Bronze Age, around 1000 BC; these inundations are now thought to be part of a long-continuing process that became more severe at certain times and in certain places.

Like the Iron Age transgression nearer the Wash, the Bronze Age floods laid down huge spreads of silt. The Bronze Age silts can generally be distinguished from those of the Iron Age that followed because they are finer textured, darker and more clay-like. Having said that, I defy anyone to date silts near the landward edge of Marshland; the picture is simply too complex for any precision. All one can say with assurance is that many were laid down by the sea before the Roman Conquest, because Romano-British salterns (salt extraction sites) and settlements frequently occur on the higher silts and roddons there.

The low-lying ground east of Huntingdon and Peterborough received freshwater from the rivers Nene and Ouse, which debouched into the Fenland basin at this point. Once within the basin, these great rivers generally had a central course, marked by a massive silt roddon, but there were also hundreds of smaller, subsidiary courses. These rivers flooded every winter and in the process laid down thin sheets of flood clay over huge areas around the Fen margins. These river-borne flood clays are known as alluvium and they often contained peats washed-in from growing peat beds further upstream. The very edges of the Fen also hid small bays and inlets in which peats could grow, unaffected by the laying-down of the river-borne clays.

So the net effect of the various episodes of marine flooding, interspersed with peat growth, was to build up a sedimentary 'layer cake'. The baking dish, as it were, was provided by the underlying rocks and clays of the Fen basin: solid geological strata of Jurassic or Cretaceous age. Then, as conditions became wetter, peats were laid down; these lower peats were overlain by Fen Clay; then there was more peat growth, followed by another series of marine floods (Bronze Age), yet more peat and then the final, massive (Iron Age) marine transgressions. So-called 'upper peats' would form above and below the silts of the Bronze Age and Iron Age transgressions. This, at least, is the general picture around Peterborough which, I must emphasise, I have simplified enormously.

Fens and bogs are not different words for the same thing: each is a very distinctive environment with its own characteristic plants and animals. Bogs can develop from Fens if conditions remain wet and stable for long enough, but they are more commonly found in areas of high rainfall, such as Ireland and Lancashire. They are characterised by plants which thrive in peats where nutrients are very scarce. In some instances the plants turn to desperate measures for nourishment. The sundew, for example, ensnares small insects on its sticky leaves. The Venus flytrap (not a native of Britain) is another well-known carnivorous plant and it is interesting to note that the carnivorous pitcher plants of North America now grow wild in Irish bogs. I have one in a pot on the windowsill which effectively controls the flies and even the wasps in my study.

Fens generally form in wetlands fed by groundwater which is often rich in lime and other mineral nutrients, so there are no carnivorous plants. Instead fen vegetation is usually far larger than that of bogs and includes many species of wet-loving trees, shrubs, reeds, rushes and so on. By and large the ecology of a fen is fairly robust and resilient, and unlike bogs can tolerate the activities of man (excepting, of course, wholesale drainage) without too much resentment. Once cleared of tree cover, for instance, a fen can be managed for hay and grazing – or indeed for reed and sedge for thatching, as at the modern nature reserve at Wicken Fen, near Ely. Fen peat, however, is less sought-after for fuel than the finer-textured Sphagnum mosses of bogs. Having said that, there is abundant evidence for the cutting of fen peats in Norfolk and north-west Cambridgeshire. The Norfolk Broads owe their very existence to medieval peat-cutting. The Broads, incidentally, are a rare example where man's over-exploitation of the environment has had a largely beneficial effect – although pleasure craft and general pollution are now undoing much of that good.

Before its drainage around 1850, the largest body of freshwater in England was Whittlesey Mere, located in fenland immediately south of the small market town of the same name. The town sits on its own natural clay 'island' just to the east of Peterborough. Whittlesey Mere was reputed to be no deeper than 2m (6.5ft), but it illustrates well the sort of closed freshwater environment that could be found along the fringe of the Fen-edge. The great mere was fed by the waters of the Nene which passed by its northern boundary. In medieval times the mere was a vital part of the Fen transport system. Huge limestone blocks from the quarries at Barnack near Stamford were shipped to their eventual destinations at places like Ely and Cambridge via Whittlesey Mere. Sometimes the barges ran aground in the shallow water and huge, neatly dressed blocks of stone were pushed overboard to free the vessel. I can well remember the first one I encountered on a foggy day in December. I almost jumped out of my skin.

The low-lying freshwater wetlands of the southern and western Fens supported a typical fen vegetation, characterised by willow and alder trees, shrubs such as guelder rose or buckthorn and a huge variety of marginal (i.e. damp- or shallow water-loving) and aquatic herbs, such as reeds, rushes, sedges, pondweeds and water lilies. The undulating marshy zone at the very landward edge of Fenland is difficult to map with any precision, largely because of the effects of recent drainage. Where the ground is sloping steeply, the transition from fen to dryland is likely to be quite sharp and straightforward to discern. But in the Peterborough area the slope is almost negligible and the boundary between wet and dry at any given time is very hard to pin down. Often the distribution of certain types of archaeological feature, such as houses, is the only guide as to which land was habitable – and which wasn't – at any given period.

Finally, I am often asked (and not just by the usual pedants who seem to plague archaeology) about the use, or non-use, of the initial capital letter in 'Fen' or 'Fenland'. I use it to denote a particular fen or feature of the fen within the Lincolnshire and East Anglian Fenlands. Thus: 'the Peterborough Fen-edge', as opposed to: 'vegetation characteristic of the fen-edge'.

FENLAND DRAINAGE

The story of the draining of the Fens has traditionally been told as an account of man's victory over nature. Sadly I now firmly believe it has been a short-term victory – if indeed it ever was a victory. Was the industrialisation of an extraordinarily diverse natural landscape necessarily a good thing? On the whole I think not, especially given the now unarguable effects of global warming which have been so clearly stated in a recent official report *Climate Change Scenarios for the UK*.★ The sub-title of Sir Harry Godwin's 'Fenland: its ancient past and *uncertain* future' (my italics) can now be rewritten, because its future is absolutely certain. Before the end of the present century large areas of the Fens will have to be abandoned to the sea. And that's an end to the matter.

It is sometimes said that the Romans first drained the Fens. This is not true. The last two or three centuries before Christ had witnessed massive marine transgressions around the Wash that laid down the Iron Age silts of Marshland. This period of increased marine activity was followed by one of relative tranquility in which settlements and salt-extraction sites of the early Roman period (first and second centuries AD) appeared on the higher Iron Age silts and natural islands. These settlers were probably not immigrants from Rome, but local 'native' British families, supplemented perhaps by a few retired soldiers from abroad. Some archaeologists are of the opinion that Fenland was part of a huge Imperial Roman estate, largely inhabited by military veterans and their families. However, I find this notion rather odd. It seems to me that the Romano-British colonists were simply taking advantage of favourable natural conditions and, when ground water levels rose again in the third century AD, they moved on.

The early post-Roman use of the Fens was restricted, largely because of wetness, but the recent Fenland Survey has found much evidence for later Saxon and Saxo-Norman exploitation of the Fen and its margins. Laying aside the situation further north of Peterborough, in Lincolnshire, it would appear that the Saxon settlement of the central Fenland seems to have been largely opportunistic. Having said that, David Hall (of the Fenland Survey) has convincingly suggested there was large-scale settlement of the wetlands west of Wisbech, which were embanked and drained for the purpose.

In medieval times communities by and large carried out piecemeal drainage of marginally wet land; there was no large-scale attempt at drainage or flood prevention, apart from Prior Morton of Ely's extraordinary and pioneering canalisation of the River Nene north of Whittlesey in the last decade of the fifteenth century.

★*UKCIP02 Scientific Report*, April 2002

The main drainage of the Fens is a story that has been definitively described by Professor Darby in his book, *The Drainage of the Fens* (1948), and more recently in his *The Changing Fenland* (1983). At this point I should also mention the book by David Hall and John Coles which is essential reading for anyone with an interest in the history or prehistory of the Fens. *Fenland Survey: an Essay in Landscape and Persistence* (English Heritage Archaeological Report No. 1, 1994) appeared three years after my first book on Flag Fen. It summarises the results of the great Fenland Survey project of 1981-88, but also draws together much earlier work. Having read it, one is left in little doubt that the Fens are perhaps the most remarkably rich and diverse archaeological landscape in England. The only other contender is the Salisbury Plain Military Training Area.* In the Fens archaeological remains were preserved by peat, water, marine deposits and alluvium. In the Salisbury Plain Training Area the job was effectively done by tanks and guns. In both instances the greatest threat posed to the survival of remarkable archaeological features was, and is, modern intensive arable farming.

The early drainage work took place before and after the English Civil War and was masterminded by the great engineer Cornelius Vermuyden. Vermuyden realised that the water from the uplands around the Fens had to be taken across the Fen basin as quickly as possible and its outfall into the sea had to be clear and unimpeded. Never before had anyone in Britain attempted to drain so large an area of peatland as the southern Fens; Vermuyden achieved this by diverting the waters of the River Ouse into an entirely new channel, the Old Bedford River. This ameliorated the flooding to a great extent, but after the Civil War the old problems resumed and yet another massive channel was constructed alongside the Old Bedford River. Perhaps predictably it was named the New Bedford River. Even today, when conditions become particularly wet, and water cannot readily be released into the North Sea, the land between the two Bedford rivers, known as washland, is deliberately flooded and acts as a temporary holding reservoir.

Fenmen have a reputation, probably unjustified, for being fierce; locally, indeed, they were known as 'Fen Tigers' in Cambridgeshire; across the county line, in south Lincolnshire, they acquired the less salubrious-sounding name of 'yellow-bellies'. In the early seventeenth century, as the wetlands began to be tamed, they complained vociferously and sabotaged dykes, sluices and other works of the gentlemen 'improvers'. It is hard not to sympathise with them, for their traditional independent way of life was being destroyed. Their fishing and fowling grounds were taken over by sheep and cattle, while seasonally flooded common land and turbaries (peat-cutting lands) were drained and given to other people, often from outside the area.

---

*David McOmish, David Field and Graham Brown, *The Field Archaeology of the Salisbury Plain Training Area* (English Heritage, Swindon, 2002)

The history of the last 300 years of Fen drainage is essentially a race between technology and erosion, and one must wonder where it will end. Problems are caused by the phenomenon known as 'peat shrinkage'. Peat is stable when in its natural, wet, condition; but once water is removed, the fibrous black peat changes colour to a reddish-brown, as it begins to dry out, break down and oxidise. The process is known as humification: plant fibres lose their strength and the peat becomes light and fluffy; ploughing humified peat land on windy days simply causes the peat to blow away. Several times our excavations at Fengate were covered with seed corn and granular fertiliser after a particularly strong 'Fen blow'.

So peat 'shrinkage' is more strictly speaking 'wastage' and is due to erosion and oxidation. Nonetheless its effects can be devastating: at Flag Fen we have erected a post illustrating the various Fen surface levels and visitors can see that the modern ground level is the same as that in early Roman times; a century ago it would have been at least 2m (6.5ft) higher. The process is seen to better effect in Holme Fen, in much deeper peat land. Here a cast-iron post reputedly (but improbably) removed from the Crystal Palace site in 1852, was sunk through the peat and fixed onto oak piles which were in turn driven into the solid clay beneath, such that the top of the iron pillar was precisely level with the ground surface (4). Nearby Whittlesey Mere had just been drained, and although the land

4 The Holme Fen post, near Peterborough. The top of this cast iron post was level with the ground around 1850. Since then the peaty land around has 'shrunk' due to the effects of drainage

at Holme Fen was woodland, and not regularly ploughed, nevertheless the top of the post is now some 4m (about 12.5ft) above ground level. Peat wastage is to all intents and purposes irreversible: the 2m (6.5ft) of peat lost at Flag Fen in the last century would probably take 2,000 years to regrow, provided, that is, the land was allowed to revert to its original state.

In the eighteenth century, windmills, often in groups of six or ten or more, operated scoop-wheels, which lifted water from the dykes into the embanked rivers which flowed well above the level of the surrounding land. By the early nineteenth century the land surface continued to drop, as peat wastage maintained its inexorable process; soon windmills were barely able to cope. The introduction of the steam engine just saved the hour: huge beam-engine pumps were installed to replace banks of windmills.★

At first the new technology proved very effective. This was the period when the large meres of Fenland, such as Soham and Whittlesey were drained. Soon more efficient steam pumps were required and these too began to feel the strain. In the twentieth century steam was replaced by diesel and diesel in turn by submersible electric pumps. By now, however, there is relatively little peat left to 'shrink'. Today most dykes are maintained almost dry, largely because it is cheaper to work this way. It uses less electricity. In Holland, on the other hand, drains are carefully kept full of water to prevent the peats from eroding away. In Fenland, trees and hedges are removed from dyke brinks to facilitate mechanical dredging which has to be carried out at regular intervals because dry or frozen soil soon blows in from the open land around. As the drainage dykes are cleaned out, they grow deeper and the land around becomes yet drier. So the vicious circle continues.

Prior to the widespread drainage of the seventeenth century, the undrained Fen was exploited in a variety of ways, which will be discussed in subsequent chapters, but they can be reduced to the bare essentials of life: fuel (wood and peat), food (fish, fowl and grazing) and shelter (reed and sedge thatch). The early drained Fen was also exploited in an 'environmentally friendly' way: geese and ducks were lured into decoys, willows were pollarded for basket and hurdle osiers and sedge was grown in huge managed sedge beds.

'BOG OAKS'

Perhaps the most dramatic illustration of the way drying out is affecting the Fens is provided by 'bog oaks' (5). Fenland 'bog oaks' rarely come from bogs and are by no means always oaks; they are trees which have either been drowned when the

---

★Richard L. Hills, *Machines, Mills and Uncountable Costly Necessities: a short history of the drainage of the Fens* (Goose and Son, Norwich, 1967)

5 A large prehistoric 'bog oak' dragged from agricultural land in Newborough Fen, north of Peterborough. Bog 'oaks' are frequently pine trees, but this example is actually oak

Fen began to form and were subsequently preserved in the airless, waterlogged conditions, or else they are trees (often Scots pine) which were growing in the fen deposits, during a dry spell. They become snagged on ploughs and can be very dangerous to the farmer. Some of the largest bog oaks – true oaks in this case – can be seen around the edges of fields that are on land once occupied by Whittlesey Mere and its surrounding fen. Radiocarbon dating has shown that some of the Whittlesey Mere bog oaks are 6,000 years old.

I can remember driving around the lanes of the Holme Fen basin (where Whittlesey Mere once was) in the 1970s and seeing dozens of bog oaks being pulled from the ground. Today the 'harvest' is much poorer and a vitally important scientific resource is being sacrificed in favour of drainage. This is because the growth-rings of the drowned trees can provide tree-ring scientists (dendrochronologists) with an accurate record of long-lost seasonal patterns of rainfall. We will see later how the width of annual growth rings in oak will reflect the wetness of past growing seasons.

WETTING THE WETLANDS

Most informed opinion today would take a balanced view of the drainage question, weighing the 'pros' of conservation against the 'cons' of agriculture.

In the 1970s and '80s, however, the cheap food argument would have prevailed absolutely: it was argued that one cannot have low cost, plentiful supplies of food and retain the traditional British countryside. Fenland soils are amongst the richest anywhere in Europe so, the argument went, it makes economic sense to drain them efficiently. Today we realise that this policy has had, and is having, disastrous consequences on every aspect of the environment, but archaeology is seldom included in the reckoning. It is sometimes possible to repair damage to the natural environment (though many things such as small-scale species diversity are already damaged beyond recall). But archaeological sites are the product of our own species, and like the people who made them, each one is unique and irreplaceable; unfortunately these sites are being destroyed or damaged permanently, either by deep ploughing or land drainage. And it's happening throughout Britain. Indeed, these are the two greatest threats to our nation's archaeological heritage.*

But there is a dilemma in the Fens. Deep ploughing and drainage are destroying countless waterlogged and well-preserved sites, but these forces are also revealing new ones, either through peat or soil erosion or by exposure in dykesides. Many hundreds of new sites were discovered in the Fenland Survey of 1981–88, and most are suffering the ill-effects of drainage. So is it possible to re-wet them? The short answer is probably no. When a site has been pumped dry it is usually too late to do anything about it, other than a last-minute salvage excavation. Once peat begins to humify, the process is hard to arrest: it cracks and loses cohesion and the nutrient-rich (mainly nitrate) waters that percolate through it feed the newly-arrived micro-organisms. Indeed, once dried beyond a certain point, peat will actually repel water.

Sometimes one can anticipate events and take preventative action. In Somerset, for example, archaeologists working in close co-operation with the Nature Conservancy Council have preserved a length of the Neolithic Sweet Track (at 3807 BC the world's oldest surviving trackway) in a nature reserve deep within the Levels. Sadly that is a rare success story. In 1986 we realised that even the lowest-lying parts of Flag Fen were being adversely affected by drainage, so we approached the landowners, Anglian Water Services, as they then were, in an attempt to do something about it. They very kindly leased us, at a peppercorn rent, the land we considered to be wettest, yet most at risk from drainage. Then we set about building an artificial lake.

The land around Flag Fen has been used for many years to provide settling-out beds for sewage sludge, and this is done by creating shallow basins, known as 'lagoons', within low soil banks, perhaps 1m (3.25ft) high. Sludge is then pumped in and after a few months the water evaporates and the land can be ploughed and sowed. We had observed this process for some time and decided to try a variant

---

*State of the Historic Environment Report, 2002 (English Heritage)

of it ourselves. A machine was hired, and a low, but substantial, bank was erected around the area we wanted to flood. The next step was to borrow an enormous pump from Anglian Water and to start pumping from the nearby dyke. The embanked 'lagoon' began to fill quite rapidly. At the time, I reckoned it would require at least ten hours to fill completely, so I went home for the night.

Next morning I arrived at Flag Fen and to my surprise saw that the lagoon was no wetter than I had left it on the previous afternoon; if anything it was slightly drier. I then visited the archaeological excavation nearby. It was a metre or more below the much hoped-for new 'lagoon' and I was horrified to see water literally squirting from cracks in the trench sides into the excavation: a few posts protruded above the turbulent waters, much as they might have done in the Bronze Age. The farmer's field next door was looking distinctly damp and the normally dry dyke between it and our land was full. The operation had been an unqualified disaster.

We waited for three days for the waters to subside and I took advice from John Green, a long-time and highly successful Fen farmer. We had discussed the possibility that the peats would be too cracked and dry to retain water sometime previously, and John had suggested that we insert a polythene film through the earth bank and press it into the clay below the peat, some 3m (10ft) down (6).

6 The plastic 'skirt' is inserted into a deep trench through a low bank around the edges of what was to become the Flag Fen Mere. This photo was taken on a wet and miserable afternoon in late July 1987

It sounded a straightforward operation, but in the event it was fraught with problems. For a start we didn't have the time to let the ground dry out fully after our first attempt at flooding. The summer of 1987 was also one of the wettest on record, and I have grim memories of battling with wet, peaty, sludgy plastic.

Four days later, with the help of a Hy-Mac excavator and some very devoted staff and students, we had buried about 400m of thick builder's polythene and were ready to resume pumping. This time the banks and the plastic film below held. After three days the lake was full and the model of the Bronze Age island that we had built in the dry, on the off-chance that the lake would eventually flood, suddenly seemed less ridiculous. On that island we placed a series of fibreglass models of Bronze Age longhouses. Sadly we no longer believe in them – so if anything now looks ridiculous it must be our original conception of the site. Every time I flick through the pages of my original version of this book those longhouses make me cringe! But anyhow, just seven days after inserting the plastic membrane, the then Chairman of English Heritage, Lord Montagu of Beaulieu, opened our visitor centre to the public. It had been a rather anxious week.

7 Four years after its flooding, and the Flag Fen Mere is beginning to look as if it has always been there. Most natural Fenland meres were very shallow, especially in the summer, and were rarely much more than 2-3m deep

We originally intended to use the new lake as a long-term temporary measure, to keep a large part of Flag Fen wet for excavation sometime in the future. But, as we looked at the large expanse of tranquil water, we wondered whether more permanent preservation might not be possible. Shortly after its construction wildlife began to colonise the water and its fringes, sometimes it must be admitted with a little help from ourselves. We have planted hundreds of willows, alder and reeds, and, of course, the flower after which Flag Fen was named: the native British yellow flag iris, *Iris pseudacorus*.

Just three years after making the lake, we had large populations of reed buntings, wrens, wagtails, moorhens, geese and duck (7). In the 1990s we acquired flocks of long-tailed tits and in wintertime we're visited by a marsh harrier who sets every bird a-twitter. We knew we had a small resident population of grass snakes living along the dyke that runs through the middle of Flag Fen. Subsequently they have spread into the lake where sometimes they may be seen swimming – on one occasion with two young grass snakes in close attendance. Late one summer I saw two kingfishers emerge from a hole in the bank on the far side of the lake, and I have seen them a few times subsequently. Flag Fen illustrates that archaeology and nature conservation can go well together.

2

Archaeology in the Peterborough area

Before we can begin the archaeological story we must discuss the techniques which we used to find the sites, and then to excavate them; the delicate topics of funding and display will be mentioned at the end of the chapter. Sites that were deeply buried beneath layers of Fenland peats and silts were found by a procedure we largely invented ourselves and have since termed 'dyke survey'. Finds nearer the surface were revealed by the more conventional, and familiar, technique of aerial photography – a method of prospection that has been extensively used by archaeologists since the First World War.

CROPMARKS AND AERIAL PHOTOGRAPHS

The archaeological importance of the Peterborough Fen-edge was first revealed by chance discoveries during gravel-digging. Aerial photographs taken after the Second World War, however, showed that the small pre-war gravel pits had only just nibbled at a tiny part of a large ancient landscape. Huge areas of Fengate could be seen to be covered with a mass of long-lost ditches, pits, wells and other signs of human activity. All these archaeological features were entirely buried and no trace of them survived on the surface. Instead their presence was revealed only by uneven crop growth which, when viewed from the air, could be seen to form coherent patterns which were plainly man-made. These differences of crop growth form patterns known as 'cropmarks'.

The principle of cropmark formation is quite straightforward: when a ditch or hole is dug it usually becomes filled in by natural weathering and ploughing and the ground is levelled so that nothing is visible on the surface. Deeply buried, the ditch or hole has usually been filled in with water-retentive ancient topsoil which the roots of plants growing on the modern surface seek out in preference to the undisturbed subsoil around it. So plants growing directly above these deep, moist ancient features grow faster and more lushly, and they also mature earlier. By the same token, plants growing above buried stone walls, or paved roads, grow feebly; this parched, impoverished growth shows up from the air as a pale or 'negative cropmark' (8 and 9). The best example of a negative cropmark at Fengate is the parch-mark in permanent pasture left by the Fen Causeway Roman road. Experience has shown that cropmarks are most pronounced in

8 Oblique aerial photograph of crop marks, mainly of the Cat's Water sub-site, Fengate. *Cambridge University Collection: copyright reserved*

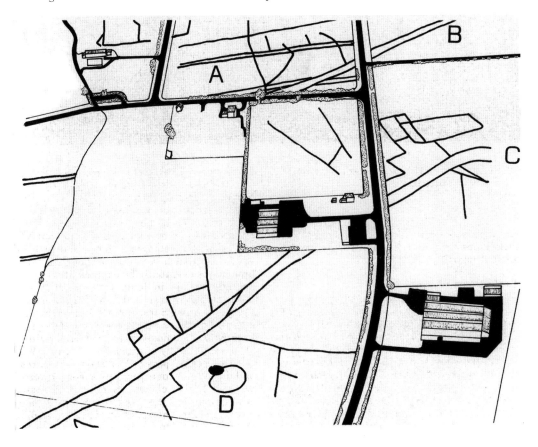

9 Explanation of crop marks visible in (*8*): (a) Bronze Age field and drove boundary ditches; (b) Fen Causeway Roman Road; (c) Cat's Water Roman farmyards; (d) Late Neolithic ring-ditch. *Martin Redding*

years with a dry growing season, such as 1976 or 1989. Cereal crops usually display the best marks, but sugar beet and oilseed rape can also be quite good; potatoes and old pasture, on the other hand, are almost useless. The nature of the ground below the topsoil (the subsoil) can also affect cropmark formation: poorly draining subsoils like clay show virtually nothing, but freely-draining sand and gravel land is excellent; chalk and limestone can be very good too. In the deep Fens the interpretation of cropmarks can be complicated by the existence of the ancient filled-in tidal creeks known in the Fens as 'roddons'. If well preserved it is sometimes possible to see the creek's final watercourse as a dark line snaking along the paler silt mound of the built-up levée (*10*).

The subsoil of most of Fengate is freely draining river gravel, which was laid down during and shortly after the Ice Age. Lower-lying parts of the site are cloaked in fen deposits, such as peat and a sticky, river-borne clay, known as alluvium. These superficial layers effectively mask and then bury the gravels, so that land at Fengate lying below about 3m (9ft) above modern sea level (or Ordnance Datum) does

1 *Above:* The Preservation Hall, shortly after its official opening in 1995. The sprinkler system is seen in operation. At this stage the wood was kept below water. Unfortunately this led to the deposition of a brown, iron and manganese-rich, silty sludge

2 *Below:* Today, the water table within the Preservation Hall is maintained just below the highest horizontal timbers. The large posts running diagonally across the centre belong to Row 3

3 Rob Fuller's impression of the post alignment towards the end of its life – about 900 BC. The view is taken from the Northey 'shore' looking west, towards the platform, with Fengate in the background

4 A Late Bronze Age wattle-lined well. The short plank may have acted as a step (scale in cm). These wells were usually about 1.5m deep and were dug down to the ground water table or 'sock'

5 *Above:* Parallel ditches of droveways belonging to the Bronze Age field system at Fengate, looking east, towards Flag Fen which lies over a kilometre beyond the hedge and spoil heap. This photo was taken in 1976. Today the power station hides the view over Flag Fen. Three ditches are being excavated and the dark soil between the open trenches of the central ditch clearly shows its (unexcavated) course

6 *Below:* The droveway ditches of the Fengate Bronze Age field system were accompanied by banks, on which hedges would have been grown. Normally such banks have been ploughed away, but in this instance one survived, beneath a much later bank, which accompanied a drainage dyke. White labels indicate the various layers of the Bronze Age bank

7 *Above:* The archaeological evidence on which the house shown in *colour plates 8* and *9* was based. The figure stands in the ring of post-holes dug for timbers that supported the heavy roof. The range pole (1.5m) in the foreground is just inside the doorway which is marked by two substantial posts. An eaves-drip gully or 'gutter' runs around the house and is drained by a short length of sinuous gully, which empties into the accompanying droveway ditch

8 *Below:* The reconstructed turf-roofed Bronze Age round-house nearing completion, July 1989, after a wet spring and early summer

9 The same house (as *colour plate 8*) three years later, in late summer, following a dry season

10 Skeleton of a young woman, aged between 20 and 23 years. Her body was placed in a shallow grave at the bottom of a field boundary ditch of the Fengate Bronze Age system, close to the main droveway which led down to the post alignment

11 Tangentially-split planks have parallel, as opposed to wedge shaped, sides. They are best made using high quality, straight-grained oak. This view shows how the spitting is done from the end-grain, using seasoned oak wedges to split 'green' oak wood

12 Coarse sand and fine gravel was spread on the walkway surface of Levels 2 and 3. The labels mark the find spots of potsherds

13 A general view of the highest level of timbers to one side of the post alignment in the main area of excavation, Trench 6. These timbers include what appears to be a dump of unused timber, including a double mortised plank (scale in cm) and a sharpened post, beyond it

14 A selection of objects from the Flag Fen post alignment within the platform. The complete jar is of Middle Bronze Age style and was found beneath a log which had been carefully pinned in place by pegs. The two fragments beside it are from the same polished shale bracelet (Late Bronze Age). The pin, the sword/dagger and the antler harness cheek-piece are also Late Bronze Age (the cheek-piece was found outside the excavations). Scale in cm

15 A selection of weaponry from the power station excavation. Below the three Late Bronze Age leaf-shaped swords is a Middle Bronze Age rapier. Below this is a miniature Late Bronze Age Wilburton sword and two Late Bronze Age daggers, one with an antler hilt. Above the hilt are two spearheads, the upper one being Middle, the lower Late Bronze Age. The remaining object is a damaged Late Bronze Age scabbard-tip, or chape

16 Iron Age bronze shears, with their carved 'shoe' box, made from ash. The shears are made from a single piece of metal and show little or no signs of wear. The blades are still sharp. The shears, which may have been used to trim hair or beards, rather than sheep, were kept in compression within their box, which has provision for a small whetstone in a slot in the bottom. A retaining pin secured the shears in place within the box

17 A selection of bronze and 'white metal' (probably tin) smaller items from the power station. The large plate brooch (top left) is Late Iron Age and the swan's neck pin below it is Early Iron Age in date. The other items are probably Late Bronze Age and include a 'white metal' miniature wheel, which may be an import from Alpine Europe. The three curved objects to the left of the scale are parts of a bronze spiral bracelet that has been broken-up. Scale in cm

18 Two shale bracelets or armlets, the upper one has been decorated with inlaid strips of 'white metal'. The inlaid bracelet is unique. The zig-zag decoration resembles that of a Bronze Age model boat or bowl, from Caergwrle, Flintshire, now in the National Museum of Wales

19 Exposing the highest layer of timbers within the post alignment. The posts of the central row, Row 3, are visible directly in front of the right-hand figure

20 The General Manager of Flag Fen, Toby Fox, then a student, stands on the edge of the timber build-up alongside the post alignment; this material includes a large split oak plank (below the metre scale). To the right is an area without timber, which may have been a small pond or pool. The posts behind Toby's right shoulder belong to Row 2

21 *Above:* Removal of the highest layer (Level 1) of wood revealed the surface of a walkway in Level 2. The scale (25cm) is to the right of the central row of posts (Row 3). A post of Row 2 can be seen upper right; the posts on the left belong to Row 4. There is a possible narrow walkway between Rows 3 and 4

22 *Below:* Planning and lifting the horizontal timbers of Levels 3 and 4. At these levels it was common to find that planks had been pegged into position by many pegs (like the plank in the foreground, right). This suggests that the structure was built on unstable ground. Many of the posts in this view were driven-in after the construction of the walkways of Level 4

23 By the time we had reached the bottom layer, Level 6, the dig needed to be pumped-out daily. This view is of Row 1 which was strengthened by an informally arranged wattle-like revetment. To the right, and just showing above the water, are two quernstones, part of a group of four that were placed below the lowest layer of timber

24 *Above:* The two quernstones shown in *colour plate 23*, as first revealed. The lowest level of timbers are lying directly on top of the querns, which would suggest that this was an 'offering' of some sort associated with the initial construction of the post alignment causeway

25 *Below:* The right-hand quernstone seen in *colour plate 24*. The stone is Sarsen, which occurs widely across southern England, in the form of surface boulders. This stone has been dressed with great skill by a Bronze Age millwright. The silvery deposit on the surface is a mineral that has formed after the quern was placed in the water

26 The sharpened tip of a large tangentially-split oak post from the post alignment. The tip has been sharpened from two directions, and the length of the axe cut-marks leaves little doubt that the woodworking took place when the wood was still 'green' and had not yet hardened, through seasoning

27 One third of a tripartite wheel *in situ* within Level 5 of the Flag Fen timbers. The original diameter of the wheel was in the region of 800mm. This location would suggest that the wheel was placed in the water sometime in the thirteenth century BC. It is currently the earliest wheel known from Britain

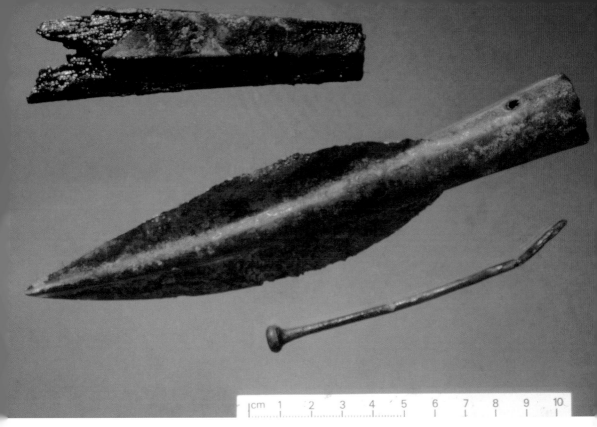

cm 1 2 3 4 5 6 7 8 9 10

28 *Above:* Three bronze objects from the Flag Fen post alignment excavations. All are Late Bronze Age. The sword scabbard tip, or chape (top), has been deliberately damaged, with a clear slash-like cut, which exposes the wooden lining. A small bronze bobble-like tip has also been removed. The spearhead (centre) has been bent and the wood within the socket has been broken-out. The pin (bottom) has been bent and its tip removed

29 *Below:* The Fengate Cat's Water Iron Age settlement during excavation in 1976. The circular eaves-drip gullies of several houses and farm buildings can clearly be seen. The larger ditches defined and drained yards

30 Mark Knight, of the Cambridge University Unit shows Maisie Taylor a spread of wood below the gravel surface of a Bronze Age trackway at Bradley Fen, near Whittlesey. The gravel was quarried from the ditch in which Mark and Maisie stand. This probable Bronze Age trackway runs towards the twin chimneys of the Fengate Power Station which are visible beyond the grassed bank in the background (centre)

10 A view from a hot air balloon of a roddon, or tidal creek near Whittlesey, Cambridgeshire. The dark, sinuous mark is the final watercourse of the creek cutting through the silts of its levée

not reveal cropmarks. In these low-lying, deeply buried areas around the edges of Flag Fen, where aerial photography cannot be relied on, we have to use other techniques such as 'dyke survey' to reveal the ancient landscape.

TECHNIQUES OF EXCAVATION

The recent huge growth of so-called 'contract' or developer-funded archaeology has witnessed a positive rash of small test pits or trenches. No new road or pipeline can be constructed without narrow test slots being excavated along the proposed route a month or two in advance. For supposedly statistical reasons that I still don't find convincing, the archaeological profession is happy to accept that such keyhole slots do in fact provide a representative picture of buried archaeological features in the area being investigated. But do they? In my experience such trenches will locate most Iron Age and later features, but they often fail to reveal the true extent of whatever it was that came earlier. Tiny test pits are of little use if one wishes to understand how a settlement or landscape developed. In such situations one needs to open very much larger trenches: a technique known in archaeology as 'open-area excavation'.

To meet the challenges of exposing huge open areas, British archaeologists developed a number of approaches. General Pitt Rivers, the father of modern excavation, worked a system of advancing or 'rolling' trenches, in which his workmen dumped the spoil from a new area on the one that had just been completed, and so on. The problem with this system was that although a large area might eventually be exposed, it was only actually visible in long, thin strips; it was impossible ever to see a decent-sized area open at any one time. Subsequent re-excavation has shown that this system caused even the great General to miss many important observations.

It was not really until the Second World War that it became possible to clear large areas of land at any one time, by using powerful earth-moving machines. In Britain Professor W.F. ('Peter') Grimes had the task of examining the sites of bomber airfields before the runways were laid; in this process he sometimes used towed scrapers to remove the topsoil before excavation. London's Heathrow airport was one wartime base excavated by Professor Grimes and few passengers there can know that their jumbo jets land and take off on the site of a highly important Romano-Celtic temple.

When I started at Fengate in 1971 earth-moving machines were still something of a rarity and many dig directors still preferred to reveal their sites by hand. Today few archaeologists would put up with the bulk shifting of overburden, so machines have become relatively commonplace. But they still require to be treated with both caution and respect.

There is no doubt that, if it had not been for earth-moving machines, neither Fengate nor Flag Fen could have been properly discovered or excavated. I have written about archaeological earth-moving elsewhere and this is not the place for a technical discussion, but basically we use two types of machine in a two-stage operation. First a bulk earth-mover removes soil that lies a safe distance above the sensitive archaeological levels; these, however, are heavy machines that can only be used on deeply buried sites.

When we have reduced the overburden and there is only about 15cm (6in) of soil covering the archaeologically important layers, we employ a smaller mechanical digger, equipped with a broad and toothless bucket to remove what remains; usually this can be done with great delicacy and precision. Mechanical diggers can either be of the familiar tractor, or JCB-style (usually used for smaller trenches), or the rotating, tracked sort, now generally referred to as a 360 (a reference to its complete turning circle) (11). A good operator should be able to lift an egg intact if he is in proper control of his machine. I have seen students do more damage to archaeological features with a small pointing trowel than a good driver with a powerful hydraulic digger.

The surface of the topsoil is carefully searched and metal-detected before the machines move in. Then the topsoil and overburden is removed. The next stage is to place a grid of posts or steel pegs usually 10m (33ft) apart, across the stripped area. These posts form the essential framework upon which everything

11 Topsoil and overburden was removed by machine. We had access to specially adapted machines equipped with wide 'bog-crawler' tracks and extra-long digging arms. This is a Hy-Mac 580C working in August, during the long, hot summer of 1976

subsequently depends: anything excavated is mapped, plotted and planned by reference to the site grid. Today we possess surveying instruments that allow finds and other information to be plotted without reference to an actual grid on the ground, but many dig directors still prefer to lay one out. It's a case of belt and braces, or better safe than sorry – and besides, modern laser technology does allow one to survey a grid both accurately and very rapidly. In the past one tried to make one's grid as accurate as possible, but in my experience it was often jinxed by forces beyond one's immediate control. Two quick examples will show what I mean.

I directed the Fengate excavations while employed full-time in Canada at the Royal Ontario Museum. This meant that I was in Peterborough throughout the digging season (April–October), but as soon as the dig closed down for winter I returned to Toronto. Frequently we would excavate in the same area from one season to the next and it was essential that the site grids married-up from year to year, with pretty well absolute precision. During my first absence from England during the winter of 1971/72 we left our trenches open, complete with grid pegs in neat squares, only to return the following spring to find they had all been used to fuel the fires of a nearby gypsy camp. Not one peg survived! The next winter I was determined to avoid a repetition of this, so I carefully hid a row of steel pegs within the roots of a large thorn hedge and then concreted them in place – a case of belt, braces and baler twine. Did it work? Of course not. The next spring (1973) I returned to find that a new sewer had been positioned along the line of my hedge which had been completely removed – together with every concreted peg.

While site grids could cause problems, the weather of south-east Britain frequently caused more: the summer of 1971 was at times appalling, and some of our more elderly visitors were put in mind of the trenches of the Somme. Towards the end of most summers mists would drift in from the open fen to the east and communication around the site could become distinctly hazardous. In conditions like these, excavation manuals become irrelevant and one muddles through, in the fond hope that things will eventually turn out OK – which they usually did.

Today, virtually the whole suburb of Fengate is built-over, but when we started work in 1971 it was still an essentially rural scene with farms, fields and hedges. Today we have Vicarage Farm Road which is lined with factories and out-of-town retail outlets. Back then we had Vicarage Farm and, better still, the weather-beaten, smiling face of Mr Tebbs the farmer. Many of the trenches opened up were actually excavated simultaneously and we decided it would be less chaotic if certain key areas could be treated as entirely separate projects, with their own series of finds' numbers, plans, maps and notes; although notionally separate, all were done to the same standards, using the same conventions and criteria. Above all else we were keen to avoid duplicating the numbers we assigned to finds and features and the simplest way to do this was to create independent sites within the project as a whole.

So Fengate was divided into sub-sites, each one of which held several trenches, which are shown on the map in solid black. It was a flexible system which has allowed the area under investigation to expand to include not just Flag Fen, but Northey to the east, beyond. The sub-sites at Vicarage Farm, Padholme Road, Newark Road, Storey's Bar Way, Cat's Water and Fourth Drove were excavated during the first, Canadian, campaign, between 1971 and 1978; the power station sub-site was dug in 1989. The Flag Fen sub-site notionally starts at the Cat's Water drain, which marks the modern boundary between dryland and wetland, but in actual fact it is an integral part of the Fengate fen-edge landscape, only rather more deeply buried and a bit wetter.

As I have noted, the Fengate sub-sites were excavated using open area techniques. After mechanical removal of the overburden, the gravel surface was scraped clean using ordinary garden onion hoes. This was very tiring but it was quick and effective – and certainly far better than trowelling on hands and knees. The effect of hoeing was to remove any loose soil that might obscure the gravel surface below. When freshly hoed clean the gravel had a strange mottled, orange, brown and grey appearance; in part this mottled effect was caused by permafrost during and just after the last Ice Age. The trick – and it took no small amount of skill – was to distinguish these purely natural or geological effects from those left by the hand of man. It could be a difficult business, and I frequently spent time and money meticulously excavating the remains of Ice Age frost cracks and ice-wedges.

Man-made disturbances of the gravel subsoil usually have a coherence and pattern that makes them obvious when seen over a large area, especially one that has been freshly hoed; but when viewed from the confines of a keyhole trench they are very nearly impossible to distinguish from Ice Age marks. Larger trenches make it much simpler to discern general patterns. On the whole, man-made disturbances are quite dark and usually have crisp edges. Large archaeological (as opposed to geological) features thus exposed are then rapidly mapped and the areas to be excavated are marked out (today we sometimes even use spray paint) and section lines are laid out with string, so that when heavy rain or prolonged sunshine eventually obliterate the hoe-cleaned surface we do not have to re-hoe.

Generally speaking, large archaeological features, such as field boundary or drainage ditches, are only sample-excavated – it simply would not be cost-effective to empty them in their entirety. This accounts for the unexcavated 'baulks' (which look like neat soil walls) that have been left at regular intervals across ditches and other linear features, such as house foundations. The baulks also allow us to examine closely how a ditch filled in: for example, was it by natural (weathering) processes or was it back-filled by man? We can also see evidence in the baulks for redigging and, in certain cases, the dry surface can be used to take solid block-like samples for subsequent microscopic examination in the laboratory. Every archaeologist knows that you can judge the quality of an excavation by the longevity of its baulks: wobbly-sided baulks soon get wet and collapse. It's a tribute to our diggers that some of the Cat's Water sub-site baulks were still standing three years after their excavation. I shall say no more.

Inevitably people's imaginations are fired by the actual process of excavation. I suppose it's to do with revelation and the moment of discovery. Peel away the soil to reveal the buried past. But what few people realise is that more time is spent on most excavations mapping what is in the ground and recording finds on seemingly endless lists. Every scrap of pottery, for example, must be given a unique number, grid reference, layer number, level (usually in metres above sea level) and brief description. Today archaeologists use a recording system based on contexts and cut lines. It's a hugely cumbersome system that was developed for use on complex urban sites and I don't think it appropriate to most rural locations. But now everyone is lumbered with it. All this information is listed on forms and marked onto individual finds bags. It takes an age, even in these computerised times.

When I wrote the original version of this book, most non-archaeologists knew little about the processes of excavation. So I described how we worked in more detail than I would if I were writing the book afresh today. In this reworking of the 1991 book I have deleted some of these descriptions and many of the illustrations. One reason that I can do this with such confidence is that the long-running Channel 4 documentary series, *Time Team*, has raised public awareness of the processes of excavation. Before the first series of *Time Team* in 1993, it was hard work starting an excavation. I can remember arriving at a building site in Fengate, where I was to cut some exploratory trial trenches. When I announced that I was an archaeologist, some wit in a JCB quipped that I had lost my way to Egypt. Much hilarity. After *Time Team*, that same chap would be asking when was I planning to bring in the geophysics. The change really has been that dramatic.

Time Team came to Flag Fen in 1999. It started badly because their visit had slipped my mind and we had inadvertently excavated what they had intended to work on. I took part in my first *Time Team* in 1997 and three years later I had got to know Tim Taylor, the Series Producer, quite well. Even so, I don't think I will ever forget the look on his face as I told him his site had vanished. Apoplectic might describe it. We had to think fast about what to do, and in the event we made a very successful film – partly, I suspect, because we were motivated by something approaching blind panic. The last scene of the film was suggested by Dave Chapman on the afternoon of the third and final day. Dave had made accurate replicas of Bronze Age tools and weapons and he thought it would be a nice gesture if we returned one sword to the waters – in return for those that we had removed. This scene involved me walking into the Mere and offering a sword to the waters, quite close by the shore (*12*). I refused to wear waders, as

12 I prepare to offer a replica Bronze Age sword to the waters of the Flag Fen Mere. This was the final scene of a *Time Team* film made in 1999. Later we removed the sword to a more remote spot far out in the Mere. It is still there

I still think that would have looked ridiculous. We had to get it right first time, so all three camera crews were called in, to cover every angle. I walked into the water and gently lowered the sword. I found it a strangely moving experience. As I straightened up I could see it lying on the bottom, a faint golden presence in the murky water. Later that day, on Dave Chapman's suggestion, we came back in a boat and retrieved the sword. Then we rowed out to a distant part of the lake and dropped it in the water. It is still there.

'Open area' techniques cannot be applied to most waterlogged sites, unless one has limitless sources of manpower and money. So Flag Fen, unlike sites in Fengate, was, and is, being excavated using a series of smaller, or 'keyhole' trenches. To give an idea of the problems we face, the main excavation of the early 1990s at Flag Fen measured a mere 7x9m (22x30ft), yet it had upwards of 20,000 pieces of wood and timber – and each one had to be planned, recorded, lifted, sampled and catalogued. In 1989 it took as much manpower to excavate the keyhole at Flag Fen as the huge open area (roughly 200msq) at the power station sub-site.

Excavation techniques at Flag Fen are rather special and will be discussed further in chapter 4; the main problem to note at this stage is that ancient wood loses most of its resilient biological 'woodiness', which over the years is replaced by less flexible minerals and water. So it must be kept wet at all times – even when one is not actually digging. This causes the most horrendous practical problems, since failure to keep the site moist is accompanied by irreversible damage. Unhappily too, dry ancient wood cannot be restored to its former state. Once dried out, no amount of water can close the splits and cracks that then appear.

So the early years at Flag Fen were largely spent inventing new techniques of excavation; for example, hand-watering via watering cans was replaced in 1985 by a splendid, if somewhat ancient, agricultural sprinkling system powered by a local farming friend's venerable grey Ferguson tractor. The trouble with this was that the water supply came from the dyke which bisected the timber platform, and every time we sprinkled the site we liberally peppered it with the seeds and pollen of the aquatic plants growing in the dyke. This caused our (palaeo-) botanist much grief, as he was not used to seeing his supposedly ancient samples sprout like so much mustard and cress on the kitchen windowsill. Today we keep the site wet using clean water from the town mains, and reflect that we live in a topsy-turvy world where the Fens have to be sprinkled with processed water from an upland reservoir in Rutland some 32km (20 miles) away.

Finally, a word about what I mean when I use the word 'site'. This is a catch-all word beloved of archaeologists. Sometimes it is used to refer to anything at hand, as in 'Please do not drop cigarette-ends on the site'. Sometimes it refers to a modern area of land: thus Fengate is a site; Flag Fen is a site. Most commonly it is used to describe what archaeologists still sometimes call a 'field monument' where 'monument' means anything old above or below the ground. Each individual example counts as a site, and this use of the word causes problems at

Fengate and other places that were continuously and densely occupied in the past. What are the individual sites, in the sense of 'field monuments', at Fengate and Flag Fen? One or two are obvious: the Flag Fen timber platform (chapter 5) or the Site 11 ditched enclosure (chapter 3). But what about the huge Fengate ditched fields and droveways? Are these a site, and if so, where are its edges? It is just this sort of problem that has led archaeologists to move away from the 'site' concept and replace it with the less specific idea of 'landscape'. At Fengate and Flag Fen, then, we are examining parts of a superbly preserved ancient landscape – with 'sites' within it, it is true – but the whole is far more important than the sum of its individual parts.

The new 'landscape' way of looking at the past makes good philosophical sense, as it stresses the integration of people with their surroundings. It also accords well with current 'Green' thinking which emphasises the unity of man and nature. Sadly archaeological legislation still protects individual, specified Scheduled Monuments, rather than whole stretches of countryside; this must, and shortly will, I hope, change.

LANDSCAPES – OLD AND NEW

Peterborough, or Medeshamstede to give it its medieval name, has always been a prosperous place; indeed its other, unofficial, medieval name was Guildenburg – or 'city of gold'. The riches implied by the name derived ultimately from the city's location at the edge of two worlds, one wet, the other dry. There have, of course, been disadvantages to this prime location: it was plundered by the legendary Hereward the Wake in the eleventh century and more recently the Victorian railway barons destroyed most of its Georgian and medieval buildings in their confident 'improvements'. Sadly modern developments have not always been either successful or sensitive, but to see good Fenland townscapes, I suggest you go to Spalding, Wisbech or Kings Lynn, three of the least spoilt towns in eastern England.

The city's Saxon past is less clearly understood, but the church that was ultimately to become the magnificent cathedral of St Peter, has its origins in this period. The region has a very illustrious Roman past with a substantial 'half-legionary' fortress within the modern city limits at Longthorpe. Just to the west lies the prosperous Roman market town of *Durobrivae* (modern Water Newton), on Ermine Street (today the A1 or Great North Road). *Durobrivae* was the find-spot of the magnificent Water Newton treasure – the earliest church plate from northern Europe, now on permanent display in the British Museum. Outside the walled town, in its less formally structured *vicus*, or suburbs, were the workshops of the potters who made Nene Valley ware, one of the most widespread and frequently found types of British-made Roman pottery. Slightly set back from the smut and grime of industry, and in commanding locations overlooking the

Nene valley, were the villas of the well-off. Doubtless these were the people who owned or ran the potteries.

In pre-Roman times the Peterborough region was prosperous, but perhaps less obviously so than in Roman times. The main area known to us of this period is Fengate and we assume – for there are no written records to tell us so – that this part of eastern Peterborough was selected because it lay immediately next to the watery Fen. Based at Fengate, prehistoric communities most assuredly had the best of both the worlds that Hugh Candidus wrote about in the extract quoted, at the very beginning of this book. In winter they had access to almost limitless supplies of fish, eels and wildfowl; while elsewhere in lowland England people scraped around to find winter protein, in Fengate it was in abundant supply. In the late spring the lush meadows of the Fen edge could be cut for hay and the wetland pastures could survive in even the hottest, driest of summers. In the autumn there were reeds for thatching and peat could be cut at any time of the year. There is also good archaeological evidence to suggest that salt, always a very valuable commodity, was extracted from the slightly saline tidal river water, simply by heating it up in shallow trays. This was happening sometime before the end of the Bronze Age, in the centuries prior to 1000 BC.

While the Fens provided a wealth of natural resources, the flood-free (roughly speaking any ground today above the 4m (12ft) contour line) land of Fengate and Peterborough provided a safe haven for people or livestock in the wet months. It is freely draining gravel land, ideally suited for the growing of crops such as wheat and barley. Given such a diverse and rich natural environment it is surely little wonder that the area was so heavily and continuously settled from earliest times.

The edge of the Fen would have crept westwards as the general level of fen flooding rose. We have seen that this started on lower-lying, mainly river valley land, towards the Wash, but the higher, landward edges of the Fen basin took longer to become waterlogged. At Fengate and Flag Fen the land was becoming distinctly damp sometime just after 2000 BC. Radiocarbon dates published in the Flag Fen Basin Report show that peat began to form in the lower-lying parts of Flag Fen sometime between 1980–1680 BC – in the latter part of the Early Bronze Age. I would guess that sometime around 1500 BC, the depth of peat and conditions in general were probably wet enough to allow wood to become permanently waterlogged, and thus preserved for posterity. Viewed in a wider, Fenland, perspective this is late in the story of Fen formation. Certainly by 1000 BC large areas of Flag Fen were under permanent shallow water which lapped up against dry land at Fengate perhaps 200m north and west of the Cat's Water, the artificial drain that notionally separates the dryland of Fengate from the wetlands of Flag Fen.

The Cat's Water drain itself poses an archaeological problem. The generally accepted view is that it was dug in post-Roman times, perhaps as early as the sixth century AD; no one can be certain of its function, but it might have acted as a 'catchwater' that diverted water from the higher land of the Fen margins and prevented it from inundating the Fen proper. Its curving, twisting path suggests that in places, like Fengate, it might have followed a natural course, but we cannot be certain; elsewhere it is undoubtedly entirely man-made.

The Cat's Water marks a convenient boundary between prehistoric Fen and dryland. To the north-west the gravel subsoil gently rises until it reaches 5 or 6m (16 or 19ft) above sea level – well beyond the danger of seasonal flooding. This is where the old, original City of Peterborough is located. After about 1970, factory development has crept south-east, up to the very edge of the Cat's Water, a mere 2m (6ft) or so above sea level.

The topsoil of Fengate west of the Cat's Water is heavily bound with river-borne (alluvial) clays. These were mostly deposited in Roman times and are thickest where the land drops away, towards the Cat's Water. Alluvial clay was almost absent on the Vicarage Farm sub-site, thicker at Padholme Road and Newark Road and almost 1m (3ft) thick on lower-lying parts of the Cat's Water and power station sub-sites. On the fenward, south-east, side of the Cat's Water, the gravel and clay subsoil gently dips so that it is almost 1m (3ft) below sea level underneath the Flag Fen artificial lake. Above it is a buried and sodden ancient topsoil, a layer of peat of varying thickness that accumulated in the Bronze Age and above that a thick deposit of peaty clay alluvium. There are hints that this last deposit was not entirely river-borne when first laid down; some micro-organisms found in it are of a type that can tolerate brackish, or semi-saltwater conditions. Today the River Nene is tidal at the Dog in a Doublet pub and sluice, on the Thorney to Whittlesey road, just 5km (3 miles) due east of Flag Fen.

The superficially flat countryside east of Peterborough is, in fact, archaeologically and geologically very complex. It conceals within its buried layers evidence for an evolving landscape of people, plants and animals. The complexities of this story have been gradually unravelled by generations of researchers, both amateur and professional from the mid-nineteenth century onwards. Unfortunately there is only space here to summarise the most significant of their discoveries, but the story is still continuing, and where there is research there is hope.

PIONEERS IN PETERBOROUGH

The Peterborough region has a long and distinguished tradition of archaeological research. If we set aside coincidences such as the birth of William Stukeley (arguably the most distinguished antiquarian of all) in the nearby town of Stamford, and concentrate instead on those who were actively working in the region, the cast is indeed extraordinary. First and foremost, although not concerned with pre-Roman archaeology, was Lord Fitzwilliam's agent, one E.T. Artis. Artis was working in the mid-nineteenth century with the flair and bravura of the best Victorians. He is reckoned by many to be Britain's first serious rescue archaeologist. I personally admire the way he removed a Roman mosaic to the floor of his master's dairy at Milton Hall, where it can now be admired by a select few on the very outskirts of Peterborough.

Artis knew the now world-renowned 'peasant poet' John Clare, who came from Helpston, just north of Peterborough. Both of them witnessed the construction of the Great Northern railway through the flat, fenny country around Helpston, on its way from King's Cross, ultimately to Edinburgh. I've often thought that Clare's memorial in Helpston churchyard, 'A Poet Is Born Not Made' ought equally to apply to archaeologists. Clare scholars regard this epitaph as an exercise in Victorian romantic sentimentality, which he would have hated. Maybe. I find it rather touching. However, the story of modern research into the pre-Roman archaeology of the Peterborough region really begins with George Wyman Abbott. Abbott was a successful solicitor in Peterborough and the nameplate of the firm Wyman and Abbott (George united the two families by marriage) can still be seen in Priestgate (the City's lawyers' ghetto) to this day. As a very young man he would visit the hand-worked gravel pits of Fengate and collect antiquities from the workmen. He kept notebooks that were as detailed as could be expected under the circumstances and have subsequently proved very useful.

Abbott knew the leading archaeologists of the day and in 1910 published the first account of his work in collaboration with the distinguished Neolithic specialist, Reginald Smith. The Abbott and Smith paper of 1910 described a type of highly-decorated and often crudely made, thick-walled Neolithic pottery as being in the 'Peterborough' tradition. The term is in regular use today. Their seminal paper was followed in 1922 by the work of the equally distinguished archaeologist E.T. Leeds, whose family comes from Eye, a small village just east of Peterborough. Indeed, the village hall there is named the Leeds Hall. Leeds published more of Abbott's pottery finds, but this time mainly of the earlier Bronze Age, Beaker style. Again, it was a paper that had a considerable influence on mainstream archaeological thinking.

Leeds and Smith might have been a difficult act to follow, but in 1945 Clare I. Fell published the results other investigations of Abbott's Iron Age finds. The work was done as part of her doctoral dissertation and was published under joint authorship with her supervisor at Oxford, Professor Christopher Hawkes. Hawkes was the senior author so his name is cited first in any academic reference – which still annoys me as Clare did almost all the research. Her paper, despite the difficult times of its publication (1945), made an immediate and profound impression; Barry Cunliffe was later to use her report when he came to define his Early Iron Age Fengate/Cromer regional 'style zone' (before the war some scholars would have used the more loaded term 'culture').

By now the Fengate archaeological pantheon was distinctly top-heavy, but more was to come. In 1956 Dr Isobel Smith wrote one of the most quoted but still unpublished works in British archaeology: her doctoral thesis at the Institute of Archaeology, University of London (now part of University College). This outstanding piece of scholarship placed British Neolithic pottery studies on sure foundations because Smith drew on material from many excavations, right across Britain. She chose hitherto unillustrated Late Neolithic pottery from Abbott's Fengate collection to name a new style of Late Neolithic pottery. Her 'Fengate ware' has many stylistic traits in common with important Early Bronze Age pottery styles, such as Collared Urns (named because of their exaggerated and thickened rims). So, what with 'the Peterborough tradition', 'Fengate ware' and the 'Fengate/Cromer style-zone', all names of important Neolithic, Bronze and Iron Age pottery styles, the region has played a big part in the development of British prehistoric studies.

However, despite (or maybe because of?) their extensive studies, none of the major scholars just mentioned cut so much as a turf of Fengate soil, although Leeds did excavate some Bronze Age barrows near his family home at Eyebury, 3.2km (2 miles) away, just before the First World War. All relied on Abbott, and his regular visits to the gravel-workings. His contribution to British prehistory is, therefore, profound.

Abbott and his collaborators had placed Peterborough firmly on the archaeological map. The next important development was in the late 1960s, when central government decided to make Peterborough the site of a New Town – one of an outer ring (which included Milton Keynes), designed to take London's 'overspill' population. In 1968 the Nene Valley Research Committee, a group of local people and archaeologists interested in the area, commissioned the Royal Commission on Historical Monuments to undertake a survey of the antiquities threatened by the proposed New Town. Christopher Taylor carried out the archaeological research for the Commission and his results were published in 1968. This report: 'Peterborough New Town: a Survey of the Antiquities in the Areas of Development' was the first thorough attempt to relate the Fengate finds to the Peterborough landscape. Taylor's task was not at all straightforward: the small gravel pits visited by Abbott used to change hands frequently and their various owners and operators were not particularly concerned about quarrying-out one area before starting another. What we would today regard as perfectly normal planning controls were entirely absent. Although he made sterling efforts to sort out the muddle, Chris Taylor warned me from the outset not to take pre war findspots too literally. As he pointed out, all that we can be reasonably certain of is that most finds came from Fengate – indeed, that is all we need to know in most cases.

The Royal Commission 'Peterborough Volume' (as it is known for short) published the first detailed aerial photographs of Fengate and other sites around the city. These were mainly taken by Professor J.K. St Joseph of Cambridge University, a pioneer in the field and perhaps the finest-ever exponent of the art. His pictures were outstanding.

One of the most distinctive sites revealed by St Joseph seemed at first to be modern. It consisted of a neatly rectangular enclosure, which we called Site 11, after its catalogue number in the 'Peterborough Volume'. It was dug by Christine Mahany for the Nene Valley Research Committee in 1968, three years before I began work in Fengate. Later I was given the task of writing the report on this very unusual – and far from modern – site, which I will discuss more fully in the next chapter.

At this point in the story I must introduce myself. Some readers may possibly be familiar with a sort of archaeological autobiography that I wrote in 2001, after the discovery of the Bronze Age timber circle at Holme-next-the-Sea, Norfolk, known as 'Seahenge'. My book had 'Seahenge' in the title as my publishers reckoned, with some justification, that *Pryor's Autobiographical Meanderings* might not appeal to the reading public. Anyhow, the book, *Seahenge: A Quest for Life and Death in Bronze Age Britain* is published by Harper Collins. In the early 1970s I had a curatorial job in the office of the Chief Archaeologist, Dr Doug Tushingham, at the Royal Ontario Museum of Toronto.

In the spring of 1970 I found myself in England with instructions to see whether it would be possible for the Museum to mount a dig there. I had no idea where to go, but had read an article in the excellent – but then still very young – journal *Current Archaeology*, just before I boarded the plane for Heathrow. In this article the editor and founder, Andrew Selkirk, had reviewed the Royal Commission 'Peterborough Volume' and had even suggested that the threat posed by the New Town to such an important area was so serious that the Americans might be called in. Of course it was very much a long shot, and Canadians are most decidedly *not* Americans, but it had set my mind working.

So in the summer of 1971 I found myself working as a site supervisor for Dr John Peter Wild on a settlement site near the Roman fortress at Longthorpe, which is now part of the western New Town. Following this I was able to negotiate a deal whereby I was to return from Canada the following year and direct excavations at Fengate, on behalf of the Royal Ontario Museum and the Nene Valley Research Committee. Thus started eight years of jet lag and transatlantic commuting: summers in England, winters in Canada. When I look back I sometimes wonder how I managed to stand the pace. I was greatly helped by the then chairman of the Nene Valley Research Committee, the distinguished pioneer of open-area excavation, Professor W.F. Grimes who had directed excavations in advance of wartime airfield construction. So when it became quite apparent that Fengate could only be tackled using open-area techniques, I found I had a constant ally in high places.

I will never forget Professor Grimes' first inspection of our work. Two days before his official arrival I had everyone make the site spotless; not a pebble was out of place. I had to collect him from the station, so I could not report to site first thing that morning. My ancient Land Rover pulled out of the station car park and we drove through Peterborough the long way so that my nerves could settle down. When we arrived on site some humourist had placed inverted bucket sand castles – and there were hundreds of them – along the crest of every spoil heap, and on either side of the trackway leading to the site hut. I was mortified. The site looked more like a children's playground than a place of serious research. But Professor Grimes, to his eternal credit, pretended not to notice. Even so, it took a good while to restore my sense of humour.

The Fengate project started in 1971 and ran until 1978. It is published in four monographs, the last of which appeared in 1984. Our team then turned its attentions to the north side of Peterborough, in the lower Welland valley. We mainly worked on Neolithic sites near the archaeologically well-known village of Maxey, which sits on a large gravel island surrounded by a seasonally-flooded river flood plain. Those excavations which took place between 1979-82 were published in 1985 (in two volumes as No. 27 of the *East Anglian Archaeology* series of monographs).

In 1979 I was invited on a lecture tour of the Netherlands and while I was there I met a number of Dutch colleagues who were working in very Fen-like surroundings. They invented a technique for discovering new sites that involved the chemical analysis and searching-through of material that had been dredged from drainage ditches (Dutch dykes unlike ours in the Fens are banks, but both derive from the same Dutch word, meaning to dig or delve). In Holland they keep their ditches full of water to prevent peat erosion. It struck me that we could do something similar in Fenland, but instead of searching the up-cast on the edge of ditches, we could actually look at the dry ditch sides themselves. We called this technique 'dyke survey' and found it a very effective and low-cost means of discovering sites deeply buried beneath fen peats, silts and other water-borne deposits. I put forward a scheme for a small-scale dyke survey in the Peterborough region to English Heritage who, to my huge surprise, decided to fund it. I was delighted at this far-sighted decision, as I knew full well that many people in establishment circles were highly sceptical of our ideas. Anyhow, that was how, in November 1982, I happened to find myself walking along a dyke just to the east of Fengate. As I walked I stumbled across a piece of oak lying in the mud. So I slid down the dykeside, almost to the water, scraped around in the ooze and came up with more oak wood. That wood came from the foundations of what we were later to learn was the Flag Fen Late Bronze Age timber platform. I will discuss this far more fully in chapter 5.

FUNDING AND DISPLAY

Flag Fen was funded by regular grants from English Heritage and other organisations until about 1996, when the main Flag Fen project began to wind down. Since then our work as has been supported by a number of charitable trusts, but most notably by the owners of the land north of the Mustdyke, Anglian Water plc. They have generously provided us with grants that allow us to carry out small summer excavations which are used to train students and others in the special skills required for wetland excavation. Thanks to these training digs, we are able to keep an eye on the preservation of the site below ground, and as we will see in the following section, there can now be no doubt that the timbers there are under threat. In the first edition of this book I noted (page 40), that '... I April 1992 will be a crucial day. Thereafter Flag Fen must support itself through income raised by visitors' entrance money. We need some 50,000 visitors to have any hope of survival ...'. I then went on to discuss how we set up the Registered Charity (No. 295116), Fenland Archaeological Trust, to manage the project, and how in 1989 we managed to attract 16,000 visitors. Well, since then we have re-examined the visitor figures we require, and provided we keep our costs to the minimum, we will break even if we can attract somewhere between 25,000 and 30,000 visitors to the site each year. In our best year so far we managed just over 20,000, so we are slowly getting there, but still have to raise money from grants and other sources. It would be splendid if we had a local government annual grant, like many other similar places in Britain, but I fear that will never happen. Sadly, Peterborough isn't that sort of place. So we must fend for ourselves.

The imperative to attract visitors did not come as an imposition, because I have always welcomed visitors to my excavations, when it has been possible to do so. At Fengate we got hold of a large site hut that was going to be burnt (13).

13 Our first on-site museum at Fengate, built from an old site hut that was about to be burnt. This photo was taken in 1976

We took a few wooden pallets apart and repaired it as best we could. Then we applied a few licks of white emulsion and – bingo! – we had an on-site museum, complete with display cases made from bits and pieces of plywood we managed to cobble together (*14*). I wish I'd had the foresight to count all our visitors, but on weekends it was difficult to squeeze in, and perhaps rather surprisingly to a reader in the twenty-first century, none of our displays were ever pilfered.

But it is one thing to botch a museum and display together when your visitors aren't paying an admission fee. As soon as you start to charge, then everything changes: insurance becomes a problem (or put another way, someone else's opportunity to make money), you have to provide toilets, light refreshments, safe surfaces to walk on, and, of course, proper buildings. These have been a real problem, because when we decided to open to the general public, back in 1987 I had no idea how soft and boggy the ground out in Flag Fen would prove to be. So our first visitor centre (which is still standing!) consisted of a steel frame, over which was spread a heavy-duty plastic fabric, tensioned by bolts and threaded bars. This was secured to the ground by a series of steel spikes.

14 One of the home-made display cases in the Fengate site museum. The cases were changed regularly as new finds came from the excavation. The pottery comes from a large filled-in pit of Middle Iron Age date (third century BC). It includes some distinctive 'scored ware' sherds, whose surface has been decorated with deep, irregular scored lines, probably made with a bundle of stiff twigs, while the clay was still soft

Then, in 1989, we decided to build a 'proper' permanent visitor centre, which we were only able to achieve thanks to the inspiration of the late Dr Ron West, of the Peterborough consulting engineers, Posford Duvivier. Ron realised that if you remove a small volume of surface silt and replace it with a lightweight material (Styrofoam blocks) you could erect a building weighing as much as the earth you have removed, without causing any compaction the delicate archaeological remains below the ground. If you then flood the area around the Styrofoam blocks you will also improve the situation further, through buoyancy. It was inspired, and our first permanent visitor centre – a log cabin-style structure – is still standing as good as the day we built it – a splendid tribute to Ron West (15).

Our next challenge was almost as difficult. Most of our visitors wanted to see waterlogged Bronze Age timbers *in situ*. They did not want to see a modern reconstruction nor a conserved reconstruction. They wanted the real thing. But now we must scroll forward a couple of years. In the early 1990s the large field between the Mustdyke and Northey road (where our current access runs) was put up for sale. It was a large area, and Fenland Archaeological Trust couldn't

15 The first permanent visitor centre at Flag Fen. Today this houses the site museum and education room. The building was constructed in the Mere and rests on lightweight Styrofoam foundations that place no extra weight on the Bronze Age timbers buried a metre or so below the lake bed

49

possibly have raised the money to buy all of it, as it was prime agricultural land and in those days farming was not in its current poor state. I managed to persuade the land agents to let us make an offer for about 7 acres, where the post alignment made its Northey landfall. Then I had to look around for cash. I was lucky. Thanks to the extraordinary generosity of the Robert Kiln Trust we were able to buy that land, which is now known as the Robert Kiln Field.

We knew that the post alignment east of the Mustdyke was under serious threat of drying out, largely because the Mustdyke itself was now so deep. This was the obvious place to attempt our *in situ* preservation. Again Ron and Posford Duvivier were called in to advise us. They suggested that we excavate an area of about 10msq, just to find the tops of the posts (*16*), because it would be highly embarrassing if we spent upwards of £150,000 constructing a building to preserve nothing! So we found our posts and then the engineers who had built the power station took a huge pile-driving machine fitted with bog-crawler tracks and constructed a 10msq coffer damn made from sheet piling. The piles were driven down about 6m into the impermeable Oxford Clay, the Jurassic deposit that forms the solid base to the Flag Fen basin. This coffer dam was in effect a watertight 'box', which we could pump into, to raise the water table artificially.

16 Excavations in the summer of 1993 in advance of the construction of the Preservation Hall. The plastic bags protect the emerging posts and encourage the raising of water through capillary action

The building which was perched on top of the piling 'box' was almost entirely supported upon it, which meant that its foundations caused almost no archaeological damage at all. I was able too look while the piles cut through two or three Bronze Age timbers and to my absolute astonishment the cuts were almost surgically clean. Actual destruction was minimal. This building was built for Fenland Archaeological Trust by the constructors of the power station as an act of extraordinary good neighbourliness. English Heritage subscribed about £60,00 to the overall costs and then Anglian Water chipped in with a substantial grant towards the sprinkling system we needed to keep the timbers wet and biologically inert (*colour plate 1*). This required the use of water electro-lytically enhanced with silver and copper. The sprays operate more frequently in summer than winter, but on average they cut-in about every 20 minutes for, say, 30 seconds. The building known as the Preservation Hall (a nod I gave in the direction of revivalist traditional jazz in New Orleans, for those who are interested), was opened by the then Chairman of English Heritage, Sir Jocelyn Stevens in the summer of 1995.

We were advised by Mike Corfield who was then Chief Scientist at English Heritage. Mike had every confidence that our system would work, but I must admit we were rather worried at first when a grey mould began to appear. Then there were algal growths on the taller posts, but we beat these by chilling the water. In the first six months the exposed timbers did indeed deteriorate somewhat: shiny, fresh surfaces lost their freshness and there was some cracking. After that, things settled down and now I reckon we will have a good display for another few decades (*colour plate 2*). Eventually my successors will have to expose another layer of wood, but not until well into the twenty-first century and by then all the timbers outside our steel 'box' will have long vanished. I suppose you could regard the *in situ* timbers of the Preservation Hall as a case of 'managed retreat', but at least their last years will be witnessed by hundreds of thousands of people.

One final thing about the Preservation Hall: Mike Corfield advised us to exclude all daylight to inhibit the growth of algae. This has proved to be excellent advice, but it has left us with a potentially rather gloomy space: black wood in a deep hole, surrounded by steel piling and above it concrete block walls unrelieved by any windows. So I decided to turn disadvantage to advantage. The Trust commissioned the artist, Rob Fuller, who happened to live locally, to cover the walls with a mural that would recreate what you might have seen, had you stood on the same spot in the Late Bronze Age (*colour plate 3*). Rob and I had several long sessions together during which I mapped out the principal archaeological remains and the zones of vegetation one might have encountered. Then I deliberately left him to it – to create his own vision of Flag Fen.

A few weeks later he showed me his sketches and I was transported – there's no other way of putting it. You see, I was familiar with the landscape, but I had never seen it through someone else's eyes, let alone those of a talented artist. Rob gave me a new, fresh and unexpected view of a world that had somehow become almost too familiar to me. He restored the sense of mystery that had inspired my work in the Fens in the first place. I hope it will have the same effect on you when you see it. Also, for what it's worth, I think it's the largest – and certainly the best – archaeological mural in Britain.

The most recent building at Flag Fen is the latest visitor centre, which this time we constructed on the very edge of solid land, so we didn't need to provide expensive, fancy foundations. Although we sited the new building where we thought it would do no damage, Flag Fen is stiff with archaeological remains and, sure enough, just below the overburden we found the partially dried-out remains of a log-road style of Bronze Age trackway that was heading out towards the platform.

The new visitor centre was built in 2001–2002 and was opened by HRH The Duke of Gloucester, the Trust's Royal Patron, in October 2001. The first official event we held there was the launching of the English Heritage Flag Fen Basin Report. By then Dave Coombs was already unwell, but I will never forget his delight when I placed the huge green volume in his hands and he saw his paper on the metalwork finally in print.

17 The new Flag Fen visitor centre, funded by the Millennium Commission, was opened in 2001. It is based on a prehistoric round house and the copper roof will eventually turn green – echoing the turf of Bronze Age houses

The latest building is very eco-friendly and is built with funds provided by the Millennium Commission. I think it excellent. It's modelled on a prehistoric round-house and soon its copper roof will start to turn green and resemble the turf roofed houses out in the park (*17*). The old log cabin semi-floating visitor centre is now the Museum of the Bronze Age, and the original fabric structure is a schools building we only use in summer. With three visitor centres in less than 20 years at Flag Fen, I can say that it's proving *very* much easier to raise large sums of money for them, than for the archaeology they are supposed to display. One is tempted to question whether this might not be a case of 'putting the cart before the horse', by those who administer such funds? Oh dear, perhaps I shouldn't have said that – at least not if I want a fourth new building.

FLAG FEN IS THREATENED WITH DESTRUCTION

We excavated sites in Fengate in the 1970s because they were threatened by the construction of new factories and warehouses, as part of the expansion of Peterborough New Town. In those rather far-off days it was English Heritage, or its equivalent, the Inspectorate of Ancient Monuments of the Department of the Environment, who had to provide the funds to pay for damage inflicted by developers. That was manifestly unjust: why should developers not pay for damage that they would ultimately profit from? So in 1989 Mrs Thatcher's government changed the law. From then on developers have a legal responsibility to bear the costs of any archaeological impact – in other words, they must pay to have the sites, which their new facilities will destroy, recorded. Sometimes they may even have to construct their developments in such a way that the ancient remains are preserved *in situ*. But what happens when there is no specific developer about to destroy your site?

This is what is happening at Flag Fen. As it is a wet site, the worst possible threat has to be drainage. And that is what is underway – and has been underway since the early 1970s. The Mustdyke, the large drainage dyke that passes through Flag Fen, is actually the main flood-relief channel for the whole of Peterborough's Eastern Industrial Area. Storm floods are a major danger in areas where there are large expanses of concrete, large roofs, roads etc. In such an urban landscape there is very little soil and too few plants to absorb heavy rainfall. So water must be removed swiftly and efficiently, along wide, open dykes. This means that we cannot dam the Mustdyke to raise the water table – which is what we need to do if the buried ancient timbers are to escape further drying-out. If we did raise water levels in the dyke, there would be a real danger that large parts of eastern Peterborough might flood – with catastrophic effects on local employment.

I have been worried about this for some time and with a grant from English Heritage we arranged for the Wetland Archaeology and Environments Research Centre at Hull University to measure and monitor the water levels in Flag Fen.

This work was carried out between 1 February and 8 April, 2002. These were not particularly dry months. A series of small boreholes were sunk along the post alignment between the artificial mere we constructed in 1987, and the Cat's Water drain near the power station. The ground water table was measured at regular intervals in each borehole. They were very dry. So dry indeed that the report produced by Hull University had to conclude that:

> On the basis of available evidence it should be concluded that the post alignment and platform at Flag Fen are under serious threat of drying out. A key contributing factor must be the drainage works ... which saw the enlarging and deepening of the Mustdyke in 1972, and a second phase of deepening in 1982.

How urgent is the threat? The answer is that we do not know for certain. I do know that it is urgent − I very much doubt whether there will be much to excavate after, say, 2030-50. I reckon the posts, which I saw in a small excavation in 2001, were noticeably drier and more decayed than those I excavated just outside the power station in 1989. We could waste a lot of time and money demonstrating precisely how fast the damage is happening. Indeed, I can think of many people who would regard this as the best solution to the problem; they would rather monitor destruction than actually *do* something to record what is there − until it is too late, but by then the problem would have gone − along with half a million, or so, Bronze Age timbers.

Of course we have tried the usual sources of funding, such as Charitable Trusts, the Lottery and so forth, and they are happy to provide grants for education, 'outreach', 'social inclusion' etc. They would also probably contribute towards a visitor centre or museum. But without anything to put in it, it would not be likely to attract many visitors. It's strange: we live in a time when communication and continuing education are the rage. But somehow we have lost sight of the fact that the act of communication requires something cogent to communicate. Right now there is a wealth of new information on the Bronze Age lying beneath the peats in Flag Fen. I wonder whether it will ever see the light of day? I am extremely pessimistic. Many archaeologists would regard Flag Fen as having been 'done', whereas in fact we have only just scratched the surface. If nothing further is attempted at Flag Fen, it will undoubtedly prove to have been one of the greatest lost opportunities in British archaeology.

3

The first farmers
(4000–2500 BC)

INTRODUCTION: PUTTING SITES IN THEIR SETTING

One of the great pleasures of archaeology is that it never stands still. Ideas are constantly evolving; old concepts are replaced by new ones; then a few years later the old views are re-accepted, in a modified form – only to be thrown out again, when the next generation stamps its mark on the subject – and so the process continues. Thirty years ago archaeologists viewed the British Neolithic largely from the perspective of Wessex. I imagine that was because that was the area with the huge stone monuments and the great collective tombs. It was also the area where the antiquarians and archaeologists of the past 300 years often did their most important work: what happened in the Avebury or Stonehenge region set the pattern elsewhere.

The two decades on either side of the Second World War were a time when archaeologists explained many phenomena they did not fully understand by invoking 'diffusion' or 'influence' from outside. For instance, once farmers or farming had arrived in Britain, subsequent new ideas, especially the earliest types of metalwork were then thought to have diffused outwards from a supposed Wessex heartland into the less favoured regions of Britain. Indeed, by the earliest Bronze Age, say 2000 BC, the process seemed to have become so well-established, that archaeologists were able to talk of a 'Wessex Culture' which was seen to have a very strong 'influence' on the surrounding country.

Today, British archaeologists tend to be more pragmatic and would only accept a given region's primacy, if it could be demonstrated – for example by independent evidence, such as radiocarbon dating. It is then necessary to seek a reason for these phenomena: what was the wealth of Wessex, for example, actually based upon? This healthy scepticism has had a liberating effect on the regions of Britain: for example, the numerous holes or pits dug into the gravel sub-soil of Fengate by prehistoric people were once interpreted by archaeologists in what one might term 'the Wessex manner'. On dry chalk land, such as the Marlborough Downs of Wiltshire, such pits might well have been dug to store grain. On the other hand, on the edges of the Fens even the shallowest hole will swiftly fill with water as the winter ground water table rises, and any grain within it would rapidly revert to an evil-smelling sludge.

Conversely, wells on the chalk will sometimes have to penetrate to great depths. The Bronze Age Wilsford Shaft, for example, was cut through the Wiltshire chalk for an astonishing 33m (100ft). On the fen-edge, however, most wells reach to the 'sock', or water table, rarely deeper than a man's waist or shoulders. So a well in Fengate would be a storage pit in Wessex. It seems so obvious now, but in the 1920s and '30s the wells that Wyman Abbott excavated at Fengate were all interpreted as storage pits or silos. In the chalk land, prehistoric pits dug about 1m (3ft) deep were filled with grain and capped-off. The grain around the outside would act as a type of buffer zone that protected the bulk of the deposit from destruction. Such a system would not work in waterlogged or poorly drained sub-soils, such as Fengate.

Misinterpreting a single type of feature might not seem very important, but in reality it was. Take the example of a well where rubbish and other material will accumulates slowly at the bottom, as people throw items in, one by one, perhaps for luck. This means that pottery and other things found together there might easily have been accumulating over several decades or even centuries, depending upon the life of the well itself. But if one assumes that the well was in fact an abandoned storage pit then it would be logical to assume that the material found within it accumulated there rapidly. Maybe it was dumped there when it ceased to be used as a store. So to explain this as a short-lived, or rapidly accumulated 'closed' group of finds could be extremely misleading, as none of the items found within it are in fact contemporary.

But there are other, more indirect, but equally misleading implications. The idea of a large storage pit (rather than a well) presupposes a permanently settled group of people to guard it; it also assumes large quantities of grain. We will see in the following chapters that neither can be assumed for Fengate; indeed, the contrary was probably the case. The main point to arise from this discussion is that archaeological 'features', in other words the basic building-bricks that we use to form our interpretations of ancient sites (items such as ditches, gullies, wells, scoops, pits and post-holes) may well be common to most areas of Britain, but they can and must be interpreted in different ways, depending on each individual site's physical surroundings and what one can infer about the prevailing ancient social context. The former may be fairly straightforward to reconstruct, providing the relevant information has actually survived in some form or another. The latter, and these are by far and away the most interesting, human, aspects of archaeology are fraught with problems and controversy. Concepts such as social context – and by that I mean the organisation and even the ideology of an ancient society – are very nebulous and depend to an extent on each archaeologist's individual perspective.

I have been working within sight of Peterborough Cathedral more or less continuously since 1971 and have, I think, begun to understand the region better than most – which is not to say, of course, that I have 'got it right'. Because of my long involvement with the area I have come to believe strongly that long-term regional research is the only way to understand changing ancient social context. The regional approach is nothing new to British archaeology, nor indeed the Fens. Sir Cyril Fox carried out a superb survey of the Cambridge region in the early 1920s. His survey area was constrained by the distance he could ride on his bike from Cambridge, where he was a student. I was constrained by the sheer size and complexity of the Fens. So I mainly confined my attentions to the North and Middle Bedford Levels – essentially the central belt of north Cambridgeshire Fenland. Detailed regional survey is time-consuming. And it often fails to produce instant results, but even so I believe it to be by far the most productive method of research.

There are other approaches. Traditionally, archaeologists have studied particular classes of sites – say hillforts or long barrows. These are usually studied, across a very wide area, such as the British Isles or north-west Europe. In my view this approach positively encourages the student to skate over the surface. This is often reflected in the end result: a well-reasoned scheme of classification that often ignores the central problem of why the sites in question were constructed and used in the first place in each particular region. So let us now turn to the development of the human landscape in and around the Flag Fen basin.

THE EARLIEST LANDSCAPE

The onset of the Neolithic period, sometime just after 4500 BC, saw the development or arrival of the earliest farming in Britain. The period used to be considered as remarkably uniform, with people all over Britain living a life that was essentially the same: small, log cabin-style, pioneering peasantry who kept a few cattle, sheep or goats in paddocks, with perhaps semi-domesticated pigs scuffling around in the nearby forest, and small plots of wheat and barley nearer the homestead. Today archaeological surveys and scientific techniques, such as pollen analysis, are showing that the real picture is far less straightforward.

The most important change in our view of the Neolithic concerns mobility. It was always believed that the biggest difference between the hunter-gatherers of the Mesolithic and the farmers of the Neolithic was that the former roamed around the countryside while the latter settled down permanently in one place, the better to defend and protect the stored grain, which was of life-and-death importance as it was the principal food they needed to survive the winter; without it too they could not plant next season's crops. It was the sudden 'arrival' of permanent settlement which was seen as being of revolutionary, long-term importance.

The new view in a way defers the impact of permanent, in-one-spot, settlements from the Neolithic to the Early Bronze Age, around the middle or latter part of the third millennium BC. That was the time when we have increasing evidence for larger settlements. But it was not an instant process, even then, and we do not see the appearance of field systems, which must surely be one of the best indicators of more permanent lifestyles, until around 1500 BC – the onset of the Middle Bronze Age. Apart from some very early fields in western Ireland, Fengate has produced evidence for what are still, I believe, the earliest fields in Britain. According to radiocarbon dates these fields were first laid out between 2930–2560 BC. I consider these fields to have been laid out to contain and manage animals and it was livestock, kept on an increasingly intensive basis, that formed the mainstay of the Neolithic and Bronze Age economies at Fengate.

Cereals may well have been grown along the Fengate fen-edge in the earliest Neolithic, but convincing evidence is very hard to come by: common sense, if nothing else, would suggest that so wet an environment, where hay and grazing were abundantly available along the water's edge, might best be suited to the rearing of livestock. But how did farming – whether of livestock, cereals or both – arrive in Britain? Was it an idea that spread, or was there a major folk movement into the British Isles shortly after 4500 BC?

The Neolithic sees the introduction not just of farming, but of significant new technologies such as pottery manufacture, that required the ability to control and direct fire – which ultimately helped the adoption of metalworking. In the mid-twentieth century, archaeologists talked about a 'Neolithic Revolution', at least as significant as the Industrial Revolution of the eighteenth and nineteenth centuries; today it is harder to share that view, because thanks to radiocarbon dating we now know that the earlier 'revolution' took very much longer to happen than the 100-odd years of the Industrial Revolution. Moreover in some areas, such as Fenland, the old pre-Neolithic ways may have hung on far longer than in others – and for very good reasons.

The various components of the Neolithic way of life arrived in Britain just after 4500 BC. The 'package' of techniques and ideas first came together in the Near East (around modern Iraq) and then spread across Europe, from 6000 BC, by a mechanism that nobody properly understands, even today. As it spread, the 'package' changed as it came into contact with different people and local conditions. There does seem some evidence to suggest that actual populations of people moved across the great plains of central Europe, but perhaps not as simple trekkers. Their 'wave of advance' is too slow for that. It would seem more likely that the process involved gradual colonisation, with people setting up new farms alongside their old ones as new generations were born; perhaps people moved further afield as old land became exhausted. That, at least, is one current explanation, but many others are possible.

The landscapes around the fringes of Europe, especially the Atlantic and North Sea coasts and Scandinavia, were less accessible than the central plains.

This meant that they were less readily susceptible to the introduction of simple mixed (i.e. livestock and cereals) farming. So it seems that in these regions the idea of farming arrived more slowly and piecemeal; by the same token, general trends are harder to discern. In Denmark, for example, it has been suggested that the huge blanketing forests were slowly cleared not to provide fields for cereal crops, but to give livestock good, safe grazing around watering-places. These cleared areas were slowly enlarged over the years, and the land was kept clear by grazing and browsing animals. Pigs can have a devastating effect on forests as they eat bark and scuff up the ground around trees. It seems likely that they were used to clear the trees, as much as to provide meat. Using pigs in this way would certainly take less effort than felling large trees with stone axes.

Similar processes might well have operated in suitable parts of 'fringe' Britain, such as Fenland. This piecemeal view of the Neolithic 'revolution' also implies that there might well have been more involvement of the original, native, hunter-gatherer population. At this point it would be as well to note that the English Channel only formed around 5500 BC. As recently as 7000 BC the hunters and gatherers of East Anglia could have chased their game far out into the damp, low-lying plains that are now covered by the North Sea. Indeed, modern trawlers have dredged up bone and antler spearheads of this period from below several fathoms of water.

Recent research into the pre-Neolithic environment of the southern Fenland has shown that areas of woodland were cleared of trees, probably by man. Such clearings were favoured by hunters because animals would be attracted there to eat the tender young shoots of rapidly regenerating plants; once in the clearing, the prey could be seen more distinctly and be taken with greater ease. This way of life is not very different from the type of forest animal husbandry we have suggested might have taken place in early Neolithic Denmark and there is no need to suggest that the entire population changed with the arrival of farming. In fact there was not much difference between this sort of hunting and low-intensity livestock farming. Things also seem to have evolved slowly. Indeed, many of the ideas and beliefs of the original, hunter-gatherer population probably continued into Neolithic times. Essentially they were the same people.

The earlier Neolithic way of life in Fenland must have been mobile, just like its Mesolithic hunting forerunner, although instead of following game, people and herds moved from one clearing to another, as grazing became exhausted. Does this then make our first farmers nomads? The answer to this must depend on what one means by the term 'nomad'. Anthropologists assure us that no people on earth have ever wandered the face of the planet completely unfettered by any territorial constraint – the definition of the true nomad. Even the inhabitants of the Steppes had to respect each other's tribal boundaries and their apparently free wandering did in fact conform to an admittedly very large-scale circuit that took advantage of resources that were available at different times of the year.

Regular seasonal movement, in which the whole or a significant part of a society move camp, is termed transhumance. By and large modern communities have ceased to be transhumant, but in the past there was nearly always a degree of mobility in most societies. The shifting was always cyclical and confined within strict territorial boundaries. Today old patterns of seasonal activity may often be reflected in the shape of parish boundaries, which in certain areas, such as river valleys, the Fen-edge or the foothills of mountains, may be long and thin. Long, thin parishes would include upland summer grazing, dry valley-side land for crops, and marsh areas for winter protein (fish, wildfowl), lush hay, peat and firewood. In these circumstances, everybody knew where it was safe to go and people were able to exploit a range of environments with absolute security. In modern Britain the only remnant of this ancient way of life is the seasonal movement of sheep onto high moor land pastures after spring lambing in dales and glens.

The Mesolithic hunters and gatherers were mobile and most probably operated within quite large territories. Perhaps each band of people had the use of a few fen islands, some open water, the Fen-edge and perhaps even parts of the higher hinterland. Doubtless, too, the territories were disputed from time to time. People would have developed various means of marking out boundaries. These would not always have involved physical markers. Children, for example, would have been taught by their elders to respect the edges of their daily world. Slowly, as the Neolithic way of life developed, and people began to exploit the landscape more efficiently, territories became smaller and eventually more rigidly observed than hitherto.

The Neolithic population grew and inevitably disputes between different groups became more frequent; in these circumstances it would become necessary to organise the landscape more thoroughly, with clear markers and boundaries, so that everyone literally knew where they stood. Society too would have to organise and formalise its lines of communication in both time and space: between different groups and perhaps between generations too. In short, societies were becoming more structured and better integrated.

The precise origin of the first Neolithic settlers in Fenland is a matter of hot debate: did they come from southern England, or did they come directly across the North Sea, from Holland? Or did they come from both directions? An alternative, more radical view, which I favour, was put forward by David Hall and John Coles in their report on the English Heritage Fenland Survey of the 1970s and '80s.* They noticed that later Mesolithic and earlier Neolithic sites usually occurred in precisely the same places and they concluded, not unreasonably, that they were therefore the products of the same people, who had adopted a new

---

*David Hall and John Coles, *Fenland Survey: An essay in landscape and persistence*, English Heritage Archaeological Report No. 1, p. 46 (London, 1994)

style of life. This is by far the simplest explanation which fits the facts perfectly. In other words, there was no Neolithic 'mass migration' so far as we can tell. This would suggest that in the Fens the arrival of farming was the arrival of new ideas, rather than an influx of new people.

The traditional, Mesolithic, mobile way of life predominantly revolved around hunting and fishing. In the Neolithic period this shifted emphasis towards animal husbandry, but as before this took place within the confines of clearly understood tribal territories. People would have moved from dryland to wetland as the seasons changed and as water levels rose and fell. I want now to examine the evidence on the ground and see how this supports some of the theories I have just put forward. I will start with a site excavated in the late 1960s before I personally became involved with the area. It was a site that I had the great good fortune and pleasure to write up, largely because its excavator, Christine Mahany, had done such a good job in the field.

FENGATE SITE 11

This site was destroyed by the foundations of a diesel-engine testing factory built in the late 1960s, but before building work began local archaeologists were able to carry out a rapid excavation. A series of aerial photographs showed that the area to be built-on was covered by the cropmarks of a rather odd-looking, but very carefully laid-out, rectangular ditch (*18*). Excavations were carried out in 1968, but on a very small scale, and this inevitably meant that it was difficult to appreciate the ancient landscape which gave the site its actual, physical context; indeed, given the constraints under which they had to operate, it is a wonder that the excavators of 'Site 11' made any sense of it at all. With the vantage of hindsight (not to mention almost 30 years of excavation), we can now see that this, the first excavation of Fengate after the Second World War, came very early in the story indeed.

We saw in the previous chapter that the site was named 'Site 11' after the Royal Commission 'Peterborough Volume' that had then just been published. It is well known that aerial photographs only reveal a small fraction of the buried ancient remains – often just the deepest pits and ditches – and Site 11 was to prove no exception. The rectangular ditch enclosed an area of about 50m x 30m (165 x 99ft) and within it there was a scatter of post-holes. So what was going on: was this a settlement site, enclosed by a ditch? Possibly, but the ditch was peculiar from a number of points of view: first, drainage ditches of farms, yards and gardens have to be maintained in a good state. Once they become clogged with silt and vegetation they cease to function properly and must then be redug or cleaned out (in the Fens it is called 'slubbing out' and the stagnant black mud is the 'slub').

The Site 11 enclosure ditch was quite big: some 3m (10ft) wide and about 70cm (27in) deep, but there were no signs whatsoever of maintenance; it was dug once, and

18 Air photo of Fengate showing the clear cropmark of the Site 11 ditched rectangular enclosure. Note also two sets of parallel ditches of droveways belonging to the Bronze Age field system in the field next to the large factory building. *Cambridge University Collection: copyright reserved*

that was that. Indeed, there were some indications that it might even have been filled in deliberately. Secondly, there was no sign of an entrance way. Normally speaking, one would expect the ditch to be broken somewhere, so that people or animals could have access to the interior. This ditch, however, was continuous. Strangely, too, there were signs of a bank on the *inside* edge of the ditch. That was odd. If this was a domestic site one would hardly throw up a bank to prevent water draining into the ditch from the roofs of buildings enclosed by it; normally one would expect such a bank on the outside of an enclosure ditch. It was also laid out, as the aerial photograph makes clear, in a very strict rectangle, with sharp corners and straight sides. This again hinted at a single period of use, as sharp corners tend to get rounded and straight ditches bent, once they become subject to regular maintenance.

Archaeologists, like other people, invoke the Almighty when they are in a tight spot. This is why otherwise inexplicable sites are assigned a 'ritual' or religious function, when all else fails. I hate to admit it, but I've been guilty of this myself

– on more than one occasion. Anyhow, I think we have good reasons to suppose that Site 11 was such a site. I still think that the 'ritual' explanation is also probably the truth, as there are good 'contextual' arguments to support this idea. We currently believe that Site 11 had something to do with the disposal of the dead, despite the fact that no bodies were found there. But to explain this we must move forward to 1972, the second season of the main Fengate project and I will return to Site 11 at the end of the chapter, when we will attempt to fit it into the broader picture.

THE PADHOLME ROAD 'HOUSE' AND MULTIPLE BURIAL

The English Neolithic has long been bedevilled by the rarity of the first farmers' houses and settlements. In Ireland there are now a large number of well-constructed rectangular houses which undoubtedly served as the permanent dwellings of substantial, perhaps extended families. But in England these houses are very rare. This is one of the reasons why archaeologists such as Julian Thomas have suggested that the population of Neolithic lowland Britain was actually very mobile. Houses, he quite plausibly suggests, would have been light and easily erected. Such a house would leave very slight traces in the ground. In fact the archaeological evidence for settlement, is likely to consist of a scattering of small pits, post-holes and hearths, rather than something resembling a village, as one encounters on the continent at about this time.

A handful of more permanent-looking houses are, however, known from England and one of the more famous of these was the one we found at Fengate in 1972 (19). The problem with this 'house' is that I no longer consider it a domestic structure at all. Yes, it was most probably a building, but not all buildings are houses.

The summer of 1972 had some long hot spells, and these made the recognition of buried ancient features a hit-and-miss affair. In Fengate we had a rough rule of thumb that the earlier the buried feature, the paler the soil that filled it. Roman ditches often revealed themselves, once the topsoil had been removed, as sharp black marks on the stripped surface, but features 3,000 years older were very pale indeed and could be extremely hard to distinguish from the undisturbed subsoil around them.

One of the great advantages of using earth-moving machines to expose archaeological sites is that they work quickly; this means that there is more damp soil exposed at any one time, and experience has shown that soil colours show up best when damp. I remember when we were working on the Padholme Road sub-site. The sun was blazing; no matter how fast the machine worked, the soil swiftly dried to a uniform paleish brown. Then one day the sky darkened and we prepared ourselves for a very heavy thunderstorm. The ground did need wetting, but heavy storms can smudge and obliterate; so we sat in the site hut, mentally preparing ourselves for two or three days' tedious rehoeing. I have often

observed that the tall, brick factory chimneys that cluster around Peterborough can have a weird affect on the weather. Storms seem to be heading straight at you, then they swerve away at the last minute. That is what happened in this case: the storm seemed to swing to one side and we were lightly caressed by about 10 minutes of steady gentle rain. It was ideal. I ran to the edge of the trench and looked down: there in the freshly moistened ground was a distinctly darker impression of a roughly rectangular small ditch or gully. As I watched, it began to fade, so we rapidly scratched its outline in the soil with our trowels, and by the end of the day the lines were sun-baked hard; nothing could shift them now.

We knew from the pale filling of the ditch that this was something early in date and our suspicions were confirmed when we began to find long, thin, blade-like flints protruding above the surface. These blades were entirely typical of the earlier Neolithic flint-working technology and I was well pleased. It seemed to me that we had the foundation trenches of a pioneering farmer's small house. Houses of this period are very rare indeed in Britain, and the Fengate example seemed more-or-less the same as the four or five others known at the time, so the explanation seemed reasonable.

The foundation trenches enclosed an area that measured 7 x 8.6m (23 x 27ft) and showed some evidence (the doubling-up of the north-east wall) that the structure had been rebuilt or repaired at least once (20). The contents included a few very soft fragments of pottery which were quite finely finished and one sherd showed that the potter had burnished the vessel's inside lip with a lightly executed fluted design. Delicate fluting of this sort is very characteristic of English

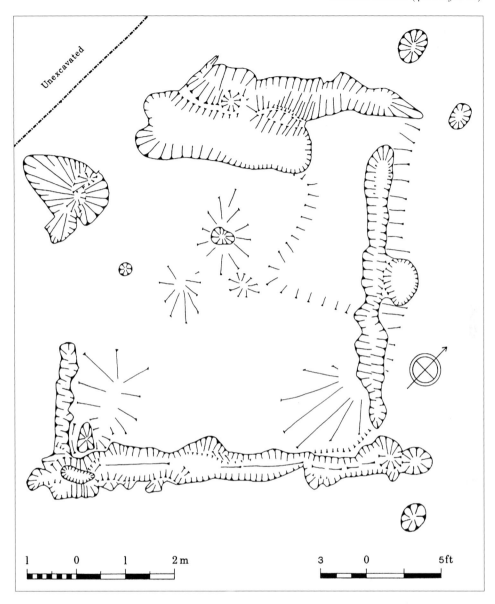

Unexcavated

| 1 | 0 | 1 | 2 m |
| 3 | 0 | 5ft |

20 Plan of the foundation trenches of the small, rectangular earlier Neolithic 'house'. The small pits or post-holes within and outside the building were probably contemporary with it

19 *Opposite:* The foundation trenches of a small, rectangular earlier Neolithic 'house'. The scale (2m) has been positioned near the centre of the structure

earlier Neolithic pottery. The foundation trenches also produced many dozens of flint implements and the by-products of their manufacture – small flakes, spalls and bashed pieces. Among the flints were so-called 'serrated blades'; these were long thin flakes of flint with serrations as fine as a bread knife; invariably the serrated cutting edge showed a clear, bright polish when held up to the light. This polish, or 'lustre' is generally thought to be the result of cutting cereals, grasses or reeds. The small individual serrated blades were probably mounted together in a piece of bone or wood to make a composite sickle.

The conventional view of the Neolithic economy relies to a great extent on the use of grain. I have said that this may well have been exaggerated in the case of Fengate, but there was nonetheless good indirect evidence for it: a beautifully made, but broken, single-piece flint sickle. The site had more surprises in store. Near the end of the excavation we found a large flake of polished greenstone that had been deliberately struck off a polished stone axe. The stone used to make the axe derived from known Neolithic quarries on the other side of the country at Langdale in Cumbria. The most unusual find, however, was quite small and seemingly insignificant. It was a polished jet bead with a low collar at each end and a hole running through the middle. At some point this cherished item had split straight down the middle, but instead of throwing it away the owner had carefully (but rather crudely) chipped another small hole, thereby converting the split half-bead into a sort of toggle.

At the time we dug it, archaeological opinion generally agreed with my interpretation that the site was a house, albeit a very early one, and there the matter rested. Indeed, we wrote it up as a house and nobody objected. Then three years later (1975) we were excavating in the Cat's Water sub-site, about 200m to the south-east, when the site supervisor, David Cranstone, was not satisfied that he had reached the bottom of an Iron Age ditch. It was late summer and I planned to close the dig down the following week. So when David made his announcement I was less than happy. I simply wanted a quick and straightforward end to the season. Still, he insisted and I acceded with bad grace.

Down he dug, day after day, and nothing was found, just bucketful after bucketful of clean silt; my patience was becoming somewhat strained when he appeared holding a single flint flake. I have to say that my delight at this discovery was not unreserved, for the simple reason that single flint flakes are hardly a rare occurrence at Fengate. If one swallow does not make a summer, one flint does not justify several days' hard work. A few moments later I heard a whoop of satisfaction: at the bottom of his by now huge hole he had come across human bones. When cleaned up, the pit could be seen to contain the crouched body of a young man who had been killed by an arrow whose leaf-shaped flint head still lay lodged between his eighth and ninth ribs (*21*). At his feet were the jumbled bones of an infant and a child and beyond them were the bones of a young woman. It is tempting to see this as a family group, but

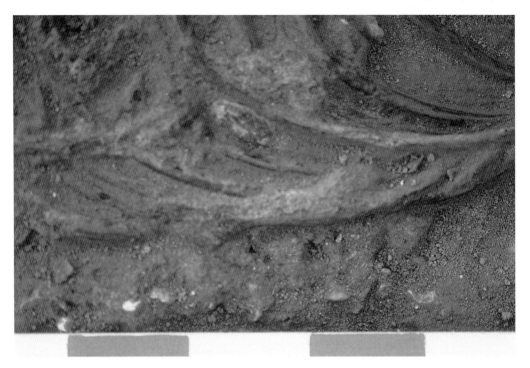

21 Close-up of the ribcage of a man, aged about 35, from a multiple burial of the earlier Neolithic period at Fengate. A leaf-shaped flint arrowhead lies lodged between the eighth and ninth ribs

it is hard to imagine the tragedy that overtook them. The arrowhead was of a characteristically early Neolithic type, and although one must not make such wild assertions, I thought at the time that the family might well have lived in the house nearby.

By now we were running very short of time, but I felt that this early homicide (it is among the earliest known in Britain) was too important to disturb. So we lifted the group intact in two large blocks, and they can now be seen on display in Peterborough Museum (*22*). The season of 1972 was rather frantic, as factories were being built all around us, and we did not wish to delay their construction. I know it is easy to take a purist line and tell the world to go its own way while we get on with the archaeology, but in the early 1970s unemployment in Britain was high and I did not feel too happy about causing undue delay to projects that would ultimately affect local employment. So we worked in several areas at once, and I am proud to say we never caused any factory development to fall behind schedule on our behalf only.

The Neolithic 'house' was on the Padholme Road sub-site, but we were also digging a large trench on the Vicarage Farm sub-site, almost 1.6km (1 mile) to the west. The subsoil here was mainly limestone and it had been quite seriously affected by modern deep ploughing. Most of the features were Iron Age (see

22 The skeletons in the earlier Neolithic pit grave were lifted from the ground in two blocks after consolidation with PVA (a liquid resin). We were guided and helped in this work by a team from the Cambridge University Museum of Archaeology and Ethnography. The bones are now on display in Peterborough Museum

chapter 6), except for two parallel ditches which ran diagonally across the trench. These ditches were almost devoid of finds, except for a few flints and a fragment of polished stone axe, again from the ancient quarries at Langdale, Cumbria. Another Langdale axe fragment was found in a pit nearby. So, with the large Langdale flake from the 'house', the Fengate excavations of 1972 had produced no less than three flakes from a source over 480km (300 miles) away. It looked more than probable that the two ditches that ran diagonally across the Vicarage Farm sub-site were indeed Neolithic in date. But what on earth were they doing there?

We didn't know it at the time, but by the end of the 1975 season, when we found the multiple burial, we had discovered most of the main elements of an early Neolithic landscape. But there was to be yet another clue that would help us to unravel the mysteries of this extraordinarily ancient landscape. It was revealed very recently, in 1997, by a team from Cambridge University who were carrying out a commercial excavation for a developer, close to the Cat's Water drain.

THE CAT'S WATER STRUCTURE

One important fact needs to be stressed from the outset. This was a truly independent excavation that owed little to me or my theories about Fengate. It was done as part of a commercial project, but to everyone's astonishment it actually confirmed the interpretation of the Neolithic landscape that I offered in the first version of this book, in 1991.

The Cambridge team excavated at the edge of the wet ground on a low gravel knoll near the Cat's Water, which originally extended a short distance into the shallow waters where peat had begun to form, around 2000 BC. On this low promontory, they found a rectangular arrangement of small pits and post-holes that may or may not have formed part of a building or structure of some sort. The finds included large pieces of Neolithic pottery, but no animal bones. Like the Fengate 'house' I had dug 24 years previously, it would appear that the objects found in the ground were not a random selection of household debris. They appeared to have been carefully selected. The excavators interpreted their site as a mortuary structure. And when they came to plot its position on the map they found it was orientated NE–SW and lined up well with the other four earlier Neolithic sites we knew about already: the multiple burial, the 'house', Site 11 and the two parallel ditches of the Vicarage Farm sub-site. But what did this alignment tell us about the landscape and the way it was used?

THE ARRANGEMENT OF THE NEOLITHIC LANDSCAPE

The key to understanding the discoveries of 1972, 1975 and 1997 lay in the writing-up of the Site 11 excavations of 1968. So now I will return to the theme that I began earlier. Sometime in 1986 or 1987 I was approached by administrators at English Heritage to write a report on the Site 11 excavations of 1968. This was part of a concerted campaign to remove the large backlog of unpublished excavations that were then becoming something of an embarrassment. I agreed, but reluctantly, as it is always difficult to interpret someone else's notes, no matter how good they might be. I worked my way slowly through the Site 11 notebooks and plans, trying to get a feel for the dig, which had been partially written-up in an interim report as a settlement of the earliest Bronze Age. As I worked it gradually it dawned on me that the neatly rectangular ditched enclosure was not Early Bronze Age, as had previously been thought, but very much earlier – early Neolithic, in fact.

I put the idea to Dr Ian Kinnes at the British Museum, the leading authority in the field and by great good chance a supervisor on the original excavation. He agreed and we are now both convinced that the enclosure had nothing to do with settlement at all. Instead we think it served a funerary function and our interpretation is now supported by the recent excavation of a closely similar site at Rivenhall in Essex; this is also of Neolithic date, and is interpreted as a funerary site, with good evidence. These sites are often described as 'mortuary enclosures'. Sometimes they were also used to house burials, but more often than not they were the scene of rites to do with the disposal of the dead. This explanation would account for the Fengate enclosure's strictly rectangular shape, its lack of obvious signs of maintenance and the general absence of domestic rubbish.

Having decided that Site 11 was older than we had previously thought, I then drew up a map of the various fragments of earlier Neolithic landscape that we either knew about or suspected might exist. To my surprise Site 11 shared the same orientation and approximate alignment as the Padholme Road 'house'. So what about this too: was it a family house or a mortuary house? Given the high quality of the material from its foundation trenches, together with its general resemblance to other, known, mortuary structures, I am now firmly of the opinion that the 'house' is closely connected with Site 11 and that both were concerned with death. It is true that neither site produced actual skeletons, but that is not particularly unusual, as they may have been used to house bodies temporarily. Perhaps the jumbled bones in the large multiple grave were stored in such a place to await the death of the young man, at which point the family was finally reunited.

I do not think it is a coincidence that the large grave pit is located so close to the 'house'. I consulted my new map and immediately saw that the Site 11 enclosure had precisely the same orientation as the two Vicarage Farm parallel ditches. Ten years later I would discover that the structure excavated by the team from Cambridge University also shared this alignment. The pieces of the puzzle were now falling in place: it would seem that the landscape of the early third and later fourth millennia BC at Fengate was far from haphazard. Almost certainly we had lost most of the physical remains of the landscape, but what did survive was internally consistent. Although made almost a decade after the completion of the main Fengate project the discovery of this, one of the earliest landscapes in Britain, was a great revelation. And immensely satisfying. It shows that archaeological discoveries are not only made with a spade and trowel.

I had pondered the significance of the alignment of these various sites and features for some time, and then I realised that the fact that they were arranged in a line running down to edge of the wetland was itself significant. Maybe they had been laid out along an ancient route way of some sort? Maybe we are seeing here a ghostly image of an earlier, Mesolithic, migratory route. Maybe, too, hunters and fishers travelled from upland to a more distant wetland by way of Fengate. From what we know of transhumant or nomadic peoples, they often erected shrines at significant places in the landscape, such as the crests of hills, the edges of lakes and at points of transition, like here at Fengate, where the Fens can be said to begin. If Mesolithic shrines equivalent to the Neolithic ones do indeed exist, they are likely to be found much further to the east, at the Mesolithic fen margins. Perhaps the group of aligned sites are a type of 'monumentalising' or formalisation of an earlier pattern of life that survived into Neolithic times. It was an arrangement that reflected the fact that communities of the earlier Neolithic were still highly mobile.

One final point arises from this latest research: if one plots the orientation of the earlier Neolithic landscape and compares it with that of the next, mainly Bronze Age, landscape, the two are clearly dissimilar. The earlier landscape does not respect (i.e. run at right angles to) the nearby fen, whereas the Bronze Age landscape does. When I wrote the first version of this book I was convinced that there was a simple, but elegant explanation for this change of landscape orientation. I attributed it to the fact that the nearby fen had not yet formed in the earlier Neolithic, whereas by the Early Bronze Age it was a commanding presence that could not be ignored. It was a nice try – that to my surprise nobody has actually challenged. The trouble is, I am now convinced it was wrong.

4

The earlier Bronze Age (2500-1500 BC)

The three-Age system of Stone followed by Bronze and Iron was originally intended to classify museum collections. Although invented in 1836 in Denmark, it has served us well, but now, it must be admitted, it is beginning to show its age. There are many reasons for this, not the least being that the transitions between the various Ages do not always happen at times when society was itself changing. Furthermore, the recent tendency amongst archaeologists to examine the development of entire landscapes means that major changes can be seen to take place gradually; our view of prehistory is less like a ladder with neat rungs and more like a clambering vine: you select the strands that seem interesting and follow them wherever they may lead. Given this view of the past, the transition from the Stone Age to the Bronze Age is highly significant if one is examining, for example, the development of axehead technology, but less so if one is concerned with the development of society or the landscape as a whole.

LONGEVITY IN THE LANDSCAPE

In the previous chapter we saw that the organisation of the landscape was well underway in the Neolithic. Apart from that rather intriguing linear arrangement of sites, that may hint at ancient migratory or transhumant routes, we still have little hard evidence for the actual ways that these very early farmers organised their settlements and landscape. We do know, however, that they were farmers and we may safely assume that by the end of the period, let us say around 2500 BC, the phase of mobility was drawing to a close. People were settling down and the landscape had acquired structure and permanence.

When I wrote the original version of this book I stated that we did not know what happened in the centuries at the close of the third millennium BC (i.e. shortly before 2000 BC) at Fengate, but it was probably important since it led to the abandonment of the Neolithic landscape. Since then we have received further radiocarbon dates and more importantly Alex Bayliss, the resident radiocarbon statistics expert at English Heritage, has been able to produce an entirely new scheme of development.* Alex has shown that the Bronze Age fields are about 400-500 years earlier than we had originally believed. She has also shown that there was no significant gap between the Neolithic and Bronze Age landscapes. This has set me thinking.

I suppose I should have realised the significance of Alex's work much earlier, but I have never claimed to be particularly quick on the uptake. I find the implications of each new discovery one makes usually take some time to filter down. At the same time that Alex rejigged our radiocarbon dates new discoveries by the Cambridge University team to the south showed that the alignment of the Fengate Bronze Age fields could be quite variable. My own team, with some crucially important new evidence provided for us by the air photo expert Rog Palmer, extended the boundaries of the field system to the west and demonstrated even more variation. Given what we know about the alignment of the field system, which now appears to have been used and laid out in blocks of land, the relatively slight variation between the Neolithic and Bronze Age landscapes can be of little importance. In very general terms they both run down to the wetland. Furthermore, it may or may not be a coincidence that the earliest and possibly most important element of the Bronze Age field system was laid out nearby (around 100m to the north) and in clear sight of the earlier monuments. This was also the general area selected for the landfall of the now well-known later Bronze Age post alignment.

I am not saying for one moment that the people who sunk the many tens of thousands of posts in the later Bronze Age would have been aware that nearby, two millennia previously, there had been a group of Neolithic ritual sites that had been arranged in a way that echoed the line of the new causeway. That would be too much to believe, but I do quite seriously think that the particular landfall chosen in the later Bronze Age was selected because of its history as a major route way throughout the Bronze Age; that in turn owed much to earlier influences within the landscape. Richard Bradley has convincingly shown how certain prominent landscape features, such as hills, springs and cliffs can exert a lasting effect on people's beliefs and imagination. All I am suggesting is that in a flat landscape this can happen too. It's just that, as in all other aspects of life in a 'waterland', everything was more subtle, less obvious and archaeologically extremely hard to define. Perhaps because it has taken so long for the penny to drop, I find this very simple explanation remarkably convincing.

---

*It has been published as chapter 16 of the English Heritage Flag Fen Basin Report

THE DISCOVERY OF THE BRONZE AGE FIELD SYSTEM

We now come to the development of a new landscape that may or may not have been arranged on an earlier, but largely vanished, Neolithic framework. The discovery of this landscape was one of the high points of my archaeological life. This is how it happened.

From the very outset of the Fengate project I had by me a set of Professor St Joseph's aerial photographs from the Cambridge University archive. These included ones that were not printed in the Royal Commission 'Peterborough Volume'. One evening in 1971 I laid them out on the floor, while my wife was out of the room. There was a shout, from somewhere in the flat, that the potatoes needed turning down, so I dutifully got up and went to the kitchen. I returned a moment or two later. In those few minutes the low evening sunlight had shifted slightly.

As I stood looking down at the photos I noticed a series of parallel lines in the cropmarks that positively leapt out at me. I looked through all the pictures and almost every one had its set of these paired ditches, although most were a great deal more faint than the ones I spotted when I first came into the room. Two sets of paired ditches can clearly be seen in the air photo that shows the Site 11 enclosure (see *18*). I hurriedly consulted the 'Peterborough Volume' and saw that Chris Taylor, too, had noted some, but by no means all, of the ditches, which he circumspectly described as 'trackways' and of uncertain date, but possibly Roman. One of the photos on my floor clearly showed a 'trackway' to be overlain by a Roman road of known early date. That particular 'trackways' had, therefore, to be pre-Roman.

The morning after my discovery of the paired ditches on the air photos I had arranged for earth-moving machines to arrive on site, for the second time that season. So this would be an excellent opportunity to test whether these were indeed Roman 'trackways'. Out in the field the first thing that struck me was that the material filling the ditches was very pale – had they been Roman it would have been much darker. So we immediately opened a few hand-cut sections and found that the finds from within the ditch filling were very few and far between – again, this was not something characteristic of Roman ditches in the area, which are usually crammed full of broken pottery.

It must have been another two or three weeks before we came across any diagnostic or datable finds from the ditches. These turned out to be two fired clay cylindrical weights, which might originally have been used for tensioning a loom or sinking fishing nets. Cylindrical weights of this sort are very typical of the later Bronze Age, and are never found on Roman sites. Things were beginning to take shape. After the 1972 season we all accepted the idea that the 'trackways' were Bronze Age, but we still had no idea of their true role or purpose (*23*). For a (very) brief time we considered the notion that they might have been defensive – a sort of Fenland equivalent of the ditches around a hillfort – but we

23 The first set of paired droveway ditches belonging to the Fengate Bronze Age field system being excavated in July 1972

soon rejected that idea because our ditches seemed to be going from nowhere to nowhere, and moreover they appeared to be defending nothing. I was also puzzled as to why on earth one should need a series of parallel trackways: surely if one wanted to go from A to B one would go by a single track, as John Coles and his team were revealing at the time in Somerset. Parallel trackways seemed to make no sense: they merely used up land and gave rise to a vast amount of unnecessary work.

THE STOREY'S BAR WAY SUB-SITE

The following season (1973) we started work on the Storey's Bar Way sub-site. The aerial photograph showed a few ditches, but chief among them was a large ring-ditch with a dark patch on one side – rather like a precious stone setting on a finger-ring. The normal procedure in such cases has always been to treat the ring-ditch as if it were the ditch encircling a Bronze Age round barrow. Barrows are usually fairly complicated sites and are therefore often excavated on their

24 Excavations on the Storey's Bar Way sub-site in 1973. In the foreground is a ring-ditch with a large quarry pit. The ring-ditch is Late Neolithic and Early Bronze Age (*c.* 3000-2000 BC); the quarry pit and the field ditches beyond are Mid-Late Bronze Age (*c.* 1500-1000 BC)

own. This is understandable, given their complexity, but it does mean that they are dug 'blind', in isolation from their landscape contexts.

Armed with the confidence that accompanies a lack of experience, I decided to approach this one differently and to treat it as if it were part of a much larger landscape. We therefore decided to strip topsoil from most of the modern field and see what lay around it (*24*).

At that time a friend of mine was the manager of a local plant-hire firm and he was also keenly interested in archaeology. He was therefore able to offer me a range of machines at very competitive rates. We had a wonderful time, using all sorts of peculiar equipment in the most improbable ways, and I was able to put together a small booklet on earthmoving, as a result. I also got to drive anything I wanted – which has proved a very useful skill subsequently.

After six weeks of earthmoving we had cleared a large area so efficiently that we did not need to hoe the surface. The ring-ditch was clearly visible, but near it (and not discernible on the air photos) were much smaller ditches filled with pale soil. We excavated these and found they contained flints and pottery of Late

25 Typical finds from the Late Neolithic settlement on Storey's Bar Way, photographed in 1973. The single-barbed arrowhead may have been used to catch fish or eels; the distinctive, highly decorated pottery belongs to a widespread tradition only found in Britain and Ireland, known as Grooved Ware. The coin (a shilling) is also now a museum piece

Neolithic type (25). The pottery was not in that Peterborough tradition I discussed in chapter 2, as one might expect. Instead it belonged to a uniquely British style of the same period (about 2500 BC), known as Grooved Ware. In most archaeologists' minds Grooved Ware is usually associated with the great 'henge' monuments of Wessex – sites such as Durrington Walls, Stonehenge itself and Avebury – and is not particularly common on domestic sites in southern Britain.

When I wrote the original version of this book I considered that the Fengate Grooved Ware settlement consisted of two large ditched fields to one side of the ring-ditch; at the opposite end of the site, grouped around a 'sock' well (26) was a collection of small scoops and hollows, many of which contained Grooved Ware. Presumably this was the living area. The shallow ditches that marked out the edges of the fields or paddocks usually had gaps, or entranceways, at the corners. Anyone who has kept or managed livestock will know that it is far easier to drive animals through a corner gate than through one in the long side of a field. For these and other reasons we began to suspect that these particular fields were used to hold animals, rather than crops.

26 'Sock' well, probably of Middle Bronze Age date, Storey's Bar Way sub-site. This view, taken in 1973, shows that the bottom of the well was still partially waterlogged. The wood might possibly be part of a wattlework lining, but the evidence for upright stakes was not as clear as elsewhere (e.g. *colour plate 3*)

The ring-ditch turned out to have a longer and more complex story than we had first suspected. It was initially dug in the Late Neolithic period by the Grooved Ware-using community and it probably surrounded a small shrine or a sacred area of some sort. It was redug in the Early Bronze Age, some 500 years later, to provide the material for a large earthen mound in which were housed small cremations; two young people were also buried in the recut ditch. The final stage of use was probably not connected with the former two. The large pit was excavated, perhaps to quarry gravel, sometime around 1000 BC. It was dug nearly 2m (6ft) deep, well below the water table, to a seam of clean gravel. Eventually the pit was abandoned and allowed to fill with stagnant muddy water and in this oozy material we found the remains of a notched alder log ladder that had presumably been used by the Bronze Age quarrymen for access to the pit.

I believed then that the fields at Storey's Bar Way, supposedly dated by their association with Grooved Ware, were then amongst the oldest known in England. Naturally we were all very excited by their discovery, but we were surprised that they were on their own: normally fields go with other fields and form part of a much larger system. Then one evening back in Toronto I was drawing up plans of the previous season's work when I noticed that the Grooved Ware fields were laid out more-or-less parallel to the later, Bronze Age, 'trackways'. Did this mean that the Fengate fields had an origin in later Neolithic times, in the earlier part of the third millennium BC? Well, that's how I interpreted things in 1991. Since then we have had to revise our views considerably, thanks to another excavation by the Cambridge University Unit who were able to excavate a large site on the fenward side of Storey's Bar Way (a road today known as Fengate).

This excavation proved beyond doubt that the fields were indeed Bronze Age, but could not possibly date back to the Neolithic. In other words, the Grooved Ware settlement was earlier than the field ditches and the Neolithic finds we found in them were therefore 'residual' (in other words, they would have been lying on or within the topsoil when the ditches were dug and do not date from the period when the fields were in use). We now realise that the Storey's Bar Way fields were a later, mainly Middle Bronze Age, development, together with other fields belonging to the southern element of the Fengate Bronze Age field system. So far as we can tell for certain, the earliest part of the system dates from the transitional period between the Late Neolithic and the Bronze Age (radiocarbon dates spread from 2930-2560 BC). For what it is worth, the Early Bronze Age is conventionally taken to begin at about 2500 BC. I think it would be stretching the evidence to claim that the Fengate fields had genuinely Neolithic roots. I see them very much as a phenomenon of the Bronze Age when the landscape began to be frozen, as hitherto itinerant communities started to settle down.

LAND-MANAGEMENT IN BRONZE AGE FENGATE

When we excavated the 'trackway' ditches in 1972 we had made the great mistake of treating them as trackways; this meant that our trenches followed their alignment. Consequently we only found what we were looking for, which in this instance were rather unconvincing trackways. I say 'unconvincing' because they didn't seem to have any purpose: they seemed to go nowhere – from nowhere. Now it is not always appreciated, but archaeological interpretation is often based on circular argument: you have an idea, you dig, and to nobody's surprise your idea turns out to be right. No, in my view the secret of doing original research is to break the circle by doing the unexpected. I'm not talking here about revolutionary changes either, sometimes big advances can follow quite minor shifts of emphasis.

So in 1974 I determined to excavate across, rather than along, two sets of 'trackways' in the Newark Road sub-site. Cropmarks on the aerial photo were partially obscured by river-borne flood clay and were not particularly informative; so I decided on the crude but effective technique of stripping almost the entire

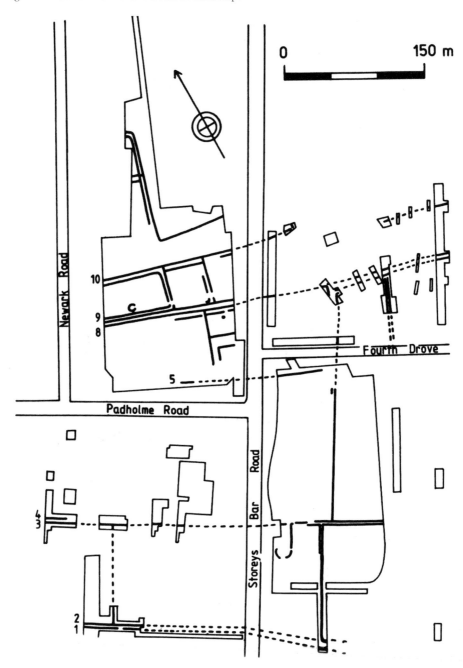

27 Plan of the principal ditches of the central part of the Fengate Bronze Age field system. The droveway formed by ditches 8 and 9 eventually joins with the post alignment, about 50m to the south-east (see 2)

field, but over three consecutive seasons, 1974, 1975 and 1976 (*colour plate 5*). I was astounded by the scale and complexity of the lost landscape we revealed (*27*). For the sake of simplicity we will consider the three seasons together.

It was to prove a huge earthmoving operation, as the alluvial clay on the surface was far thicker than we anticipated. At first we could see nothing, but gradually the outline of a massive ditch began to be revealed as we slowly worked our way down towards the gravel. Chris Taylor's original 'trackway' explanation, which originally seemed so odd, turned out to be remarkably accurate, since the parallel ditches ran on either side of a ribbon of land along which livestock were driven. In Fenland this type of track, running down to the wet from the dry is generally known as a 'drove'. The word drove also implies that the road was specifically intended to be used for the driving (droving) of large numbers of animals. For this they are usually bounded by thick-laid hedges, often set atop banks outside the parallel ditches. We recreated one of the Bronze Age hedged droveways in our archaeological park at Flag Fen and I can vouch that it is a very effective way of moving animals about the place (*28*). Recently (2003) we laid the hedges in traditional fashion and they are now fully stock-proof. I suspect that many Bronze Age axes were used for such jobs around the farm, rather than

28 The main droveway formed by ditches 8 and 9 as reconstructed in the Flag Fen archaeological park. Note the turf-roofed round house behind the hedge (left). This photo was taken two years after the hedge had been planted

for just felling trees. Usually it is cattle and sheep that are moved in this way. In my experience pigs and goats have minds that were wired by a malevolent creator: they would rather eat or walk through a hedge than be guided by one.

At Fengate there are four modern roads known as the First, Second, Third and Fourth Droves; two (and I suspect this would apply to the others, did we but know it) run parallel to their prehistoric forebears. This is not continuity in the strict sense (when property boundaries are handed on unchanged from one generation to another), but rather it reflects the fact that people living on the flood-free higher land must always have needed access to the Fen for their livestock and other farm traffic. If the folk farming the very edge of the Fen were unfriendly or greedy, it would make excellent sense, and would avoid conflict, if everyone in the community recognised that access along the droves was open to anyone. It would also make sense if those access routes were as direct as possible. This is why the prehistoric and modern droves run at strict right-angles to the Fen.

Anyhow, the droveway idea seemed an excellent working hypothesis, but we had to prove it somehow. By this time I'd had the very good fortune to come across Dr Paul Craddock who had just started working for the British Museum Research Laboratory, where he is now a senior scientist. At the time we were both interested in the compositional analysis of Bronze Age metal, for the information it could provide on trade and metalworking technology. In 1972 I invited Paul to Canada to analyse some of the Royal Ontario Museum's British prehistoric bronzes, and while he was there he casually mentioned that he had a cheap and foolproof method for doing soil phosphate analyses. I think he was a bit surprised at my wild excitement at hearing this news.

The reason for my enthusiasm is that when farm animals defecate or urinate they enrich the soil with organic phosphates; if the soil conditions are right, then the phosphate molecules lock into the soil particles around them and stubbornly refuse to budge. If one has access, as I now did, to an analytical chemist then the soil phosphate level can be measured at one spot – the Bronze Age droveway surface in our case – and compared with the land round about. Paul Craddock equipped us with a mini-phosphate laboratory on site, courtesy of the British Museum Research Laboratory, and we set to work.

The results showed that the surface of the ground between the droveway ditches held a higher concentration of phosphate than the land around. This was self-explanatory: more animals were going about their business there. But when we analysed soil from the sides of the droveway ditches we found that there was more phosphate along the top, or brink, than at the bottom. This was puzzling, but consistent, all along the ditches. It soon became apparent that the expected pattern of high phosphate along the bottom of a ditch would be the result of rapid run-off caused by poor drainage. So how did this happen?

Imagine a well-turfed and grassy droveway used by animals: the dung would remain on the turf until it rained, when it would be washed into the ditch – at which point it would 'fix' into the soil at the bottom. But if, as we strongly suspected from a wealth of other evidence (the number of animal bones found, the frequent modification of field entranceways and the regular recutting of ditches), the droveway surface was worn bare by the constant passage of livestock, then there would be no turf to prevent the phosphates in the dung being absorbed directly into the soil. When it rained, the surface would absorb the water and become a smelly, muddy mess, familiar to anyone who has lived on a farm. The liquid in the slurry would soon join the water table, which in winter would be just below the surface.

The ditches of the Newark Road sub-site formed an extraordinarily well-organised pattern, arranged around a series of droveways. We plotted the cropmarks from aerial photographs and came up with a map on which we marked and numbered the principal ditches. Only the main ditches showed up on the aerial photos which otherwise gave no hint that the 'trackways' were linked together by many other ditches and smaller, subsidiary droves; this illustrates well the very great danger of attempting to read too much into even the very best aerial photos. The ditches we numbered 6 and 7 had vanished when we actually came to look for them by excavation. So we must attribute their presence on the photo to a trick of the light, or modern disturbance that affected soil drainage. The main droveway was clearly that marked by the paired 'trackway' Ditches 8 and 9. It ran from east to west, across the Fourth Drove sub-site, down to the fen beyond it.

Ditches 8 and 9 were often of very variable depth, profile and width, and it soon became apparent that they had been extensively dug, redug, filled in and then opened again. In most instances these activities were connected with the making and blocking of causeways across the ditch. These causeways were usually at the corners of neighbouring fields or paddocks, just as we had seen at Storey's Bar Way. We also noticed that a causeway across Ditch 8 would never line up with one across Ditch 9. In other words there was no evidence to suggest that people wanted to drive livestock straight across the droveway. In this respect it served as much a barrier or boundary as a droveway. The fields or paddocks on either side of the droveway marked by Ditches 8 and 9 were laid out without regard to each other: not only did entranceways not line up, but neither did subsidiary droves or even field boundary ditches. The two sets of paddocks seemed to be entirely self-contained and were separated from each other by the main drove, that defined Ditches 8 and 9.

I think it would be a mistake to think of the fields and droveways of Bronze Age Fengate as belonging to a landscape in which livestock dominated everything. I am sure that cereal crops were grown, but probably in garden plots close-by the farmstead, rather than in fields, as happens today. Being close to the animal byres these plots could be readily manured, and being handy for the farmhouse they could be weeded when necessary. In 1997 I was able to excavate a large Bronze Age settlement at Welland Bank, a few miles north of Peterborough, and here we found evidence for Bronze Age garden plots near the settlement.★ We also found abundant evidence for the extraction of salt from saltwater. We know that this was also happening at both Fengate and Northey, because we recovered the distinctive fired clay evaporation dishes and salt moulds, made from cylindrical vessels sawn in half after firing. These objects were found in ditches of the Bronze Age fields.

This pattern of fields with two clearly defined axes has been described as 'co-axial' by Andrew Fleming who has worked on much larger and broadly contemporary Bronze Age field or 'Reave' systems on Dartmoor. At Fengate we believe that the landscape was originally divided into large areas or holdings by the main 'boundary droves', such as that between Ditches 8 and 9. Perhaps these large areas belonged to, or were controlled by, the more significant individual families. Maybe the sub-divisions within them, essentially the fields and smaller, subsidiary droves, then came into being as and when required. Perhaps this sub-division of the landscape was as much a function of social factors, such as family growth and family politics as it was a reflection of what was happening in the world of animal husbandry. We will see shortly that the role of the droveway marked by Ditches 8 and 9, as a boundary was just as important as its more obvious 'trackway' function.

These ideas were fine so far as they went, but some practical difficulties still remained. For example, some of the drove and field boundary ditches were only 20-30cm (9-12in) deep, when excavated. If one adds another 30cm (1ft) to compensate for lost topsoil and soil erosion, this still only provides a very slight obstacle for any determined cow or sheep. Even add a bank of roughly the same size, and it is still negligible, but then plant a stout thorn hedge on top of the bank, and you will have a completely stock-proof barrier in five to seven years. There is no evidence for fence posts at Fengate – and in view of the wet soil this is not surprising – so a hedge is quite simply the only way the land could have been physically divided up. Having said that, it is always possible that the small ditches were merely psychological barriers, like the drove of Ditches 8 and 9; or perhaps livestock were either tethered in place, or were constantly supervised by several stockmen. Personally, I find such suggestions improbable. If, for example, the small droveway ditches only served a psychological boundary function they would soon have been obliterated by wandering hooves; as it is, they are sharp and well defined, protected, I would argue, by a stout physical barrier.

It has long been assumed in archaeology that, when you dig a ditch and throw the spoil to one side, the loose earth will eventually slip back into the ditch especially when it is attacked by natural foes such as rain, snow and frosts. In certain circumstances this makes some sense, for example, if one is building an earthen fort

---

★I discuss Welland Bank in chapter 8 of my book, *Farmers in Prehistoric Britain* (Tempus Books, 1998)

one tries to make the encircling bank and ditch as substantial as possible, so they are placed close to each another to form a single slide-slope. Such artificial slopes are very prone to natural erosion. If, on the other hand, you are digging a ditch in the Fens you do not want to have to dig it out at regular intervals, so common sense tells you to ensure that the bank is both flat and set well back from the edge of the ditch. That way it won't keep slipping back in. It was hardly surprising that few of the Fengate field or droveway ditches showed signs of bank collapse in their infilling. It simply meant that they had been dug by prehistoric Fenmen who knew how to save themselves effort in the future. It did *not* mean that there were no banks. When colleagues visited the Newark Road excavations I would point out that there was no direct archaeological evidence for banks, but I still stoutly maintained that they must have been there. I need hardly add that I was rarely believed.

So I determined to have a serious look for these fugitive banks and turned my attention first to the nearby Fourth Drove sub-site, where the river-borne clay cover was thicker and where there was a large modern drainage dyke under whose upcast we might find what we were after. Below the thick topsoil at the edge of the dyke we found Ditch 10 and to one side of it what we had been looking for: a low, flat mound capped with gravel that had been dug from the bottom of the ditch (*colour plate 6*). The mound was placed well back from the ditch by the Bronze Age farmer who had plainly had no intention of redigging it more than was absolutely necessary. The gravel on the top of the mound showed slight signs of disturbance, but one could not say with absolute confidence that this resulted from root action. However, the neat and regular profile of both the ditch and its accompanying bank suggests a degree of physical protection that was probably, I would suggest, provided by a hedge.

HOUSES AND HABITATIONS

Our excavations around the Bronze Age field system revealed the foundations of three or four Bronze Age round-houses, one of which was particularly well preserved (*colour plate 7*). The building in question was on the Newark Road sub-site and had been placed in a paddock alongside Ditch 9. No wood survived, but the stains left by posts in the gravel subsoil were clearly visible. The building showed no signs of repair and probably remained in use for no more than 20-30 years. It consisted of an exterior encircling eaves-drip gully (the equivalent of a ground-level gutter), a circular exterior wall with a diameter of about 8m (26ft) and a single, porched doorway which faced eastwards and would have allowed the inhabitants to keep an eye on animals in the adjoining two paddocks. The eaves-drip gully eventually drained into a subsidiary drain running parallel to Ditch 9.

The building had a central hearth, but its main interest lay in a series of posts which formed an internal ring of roof supports. Bronze Age buildings often have such an internal post-ring, and archaeologists have long been puzzled by them,

29 Reconstructing the first Fengate Bronze Age round house. Here wattle has been woven around the wall posts to tie them securely together before taking the weight of the roof rafters, which are here upsidedown and leaning against the internal supported ring-beam

for the simple reason that if the roof was thatched with reed or straw the weight (in this case up to about 2 tonnes when wet) simply would not have required additional support. The late Peter Reynolds' famous experiments at the Little Butser Iron Age farm have shown that large round-houses with thick thatch and a properly constructed conical roof are perfectly stable when the weight is taken on the walls alone. Internal roof supports are therefore not needed. But would such a building work on the softer soils and in the windy winter days of the Fens?

We decided to resolve these problem by attempting a full-scale reconstruction (*29* and *30*). We also determined that we would go the whole way and reconstruct not just the house, but the fields and droveway, too. We would have liked to have done this on the precise spot where the building originally stood, but this was already occupied by a large factory. So we bided our time, and eventually obtained land at Flag Fen, just to the east of Fengate, and this is where we have built our experimental Bronze Age structures. We originally intended to go the whole hog and fell every pole with Bronze Age axes, but soon gave the idea up when we came to cost the operation with more precision. So I must now confess that we compromised and felled half a dozen poles using authentic techniques, before laying our palstaves (a type of Bronze Age axe) aside. We then resumed work with chainsaws.

30 Attaching the purlins to the roof rafters. The framework of the roof had to be very strong to take the weight of the turf. The completed house can be seen in *colour plates 8* and *9*

We gave a Bronze Age axe to Rodney Newborough, a senior forester with the Forestry Commission and he felled several trees of 30cm (1ft) diameter in about three minutes each (it takes me a good quarter of an hour). After felling three trees, Rodney's bronze axe blade was still as sharp as a razor. It was most noticeable that the trees were felled well above ground level – far higher than with modern long-handled steel felling axes. We built our first round building in 1989 and were advised on its construction by John Spencer who has built round-houses all over the country. Before becoming a prehistoric house-builder John worked with us on various excavations in the Peterborough area, while still a student at Manchester University. So by dint of persistent pestering, coupled with a degree of acceptable moral blackmail, we persuaded him to give us a hand. John was the first to have the idea that the ring of roof-support posts may have been necessary because of the roof's weight. Clearly this meant that thatch was out, and there is no suitable local stone, but what about turf?

Turf-roofed houses are known from northern Scotland, the Western Isles and also in Scandinavia. John calculated that our roof, if turfed and when wet, could weigh 7 or 8 tonnes, and this would certainly require substantial support. We knew from our reading of Scottish accounts that the first layer of turf was laid green-side down, and the second was laid on it, but right-side up. Then the two grew together to make a very solid mat.

The summer of 1989 was improbably hot and dry and we only kept the grass on the roof alive by dint of assiduous sprinkling (*colour plates 8* and *9*). At the end of the summer the turf had formed into a tough covering and, although I was able to walk around on it barefoot, it was by no means waterproof. By great good fortune we happened to be visited by Dr Bengt Edgren, a colleague who was in the process of opening a reconstructed Iron Age fort in southern Sweden to the public. He was not surprised at our leaky roof and pointed out that theirs, which may last 20 years or more, have a 80-100mm (3-4in) straw or reed lining which channels water to the ground. The turf then serves to keep the lining in place and makes an efficient insulation – which is highly desirable in Sweden.

We followed his advice and inserted a layer of second-hand thatcher's reed below the turf, and so far the experiment had proved successful. Originally we intended to keep the roof tidy by having it grazed by primitive sheep, but the dry summers of eastern England discourage grass growth. So now we have a two-tone roof: in autumn, winter and spring it's green and in summer it's brown. Flag Fen also boasts its own small flocks of mouflon and Soay sheep, very primitive rare breeds whose bones are virtually identical to those found on Neolithic and Bronze Age sites in Britain and Europe. The ancestors of our mouflon came from Corsica. When we first built the round-house we used it as a winter shelter for the Soays and it was an extraordinary sensation to be inside it with these, its rightful occupants. It was hard not to feel like some sort of intruder.

The ditched fields of the Newark Road sub-site were of prime importance, but they had undoubtedly been slightly affected by deep ploughing in modern times, so we decided to examine the nearby Fourth Drove sub-site more closely, for here, as we have already noted, the overlying alluvial clays were very much thicker. Unfortunately we had to defer this examination until 1978, the last year of the project, which was not entirely our fault as the land was not available until then, and when we got down to the work, the sheer quantity of overburden made 'open area' excavation impossible, given our limited budget. So we dug long keyhole trenches, about 5m (16ft) wide and demonstrated that the whole prehistoric land surface, including the topsoil, lay below the alluvium, untouched, so far as we could tell, by modern ploughing. I still bitterly regret not being able to excavate Fourth Drove properly, using open area techniques, but that was the way things worked out.

In 1989 we examined the power station sub-site immediately to the fenward, or easterly, side of the Fourth Drove sub-site. This will be covered more fully in the next chapter, but to our absolute delight we found that our old friends Ditches 8 and 9 ran right up to the edge of the water. This was very important, because it meant that after 18 years' research we had finally and definitively linked the dryland landscape to the nearby fen. It was important to us, but we would soon learn just how significant it was to people in the Bronze Age.

THE BRONZE AGE FENS

I cannot finish a discussion of the Bronze Age in the Fens without saying something about the impact made by English Heritage's Fenland Project. Those with an interest in such things will be aware of the many volumes of survey published in the series of monographs known as East Anglian Archaeology. I have already mentioned that a more accessible summary, *Fenland Survey: an essay in landscape and persistence*, has been published by English Heritage, jointly written by David Hall and John Coles. John is of course well known to everyone in archaeology for his work in the Somerset Levels, Scandinavian rock art, experimental archaeology and many other topics besides. David is an acknowledged authority on the medieval landscape, but like all good field archaeologists he can turn his hand to almost anything. His contribution to the archaeology of the Fens has been little short of revolutionary.

David Hall was the first field officer with the Fenland Project and did most of his fieldwork in the Cambridgeshire Fens. He started tramping across fields in 1976 (five years before the official Fenland Project came into existence), working his way through, or rather across, 8000ha (20,000 acres) a year. Quite soon after he started this Herculean task he came across a series of very low gravel mounds. These mounds were in peat country near the village of Haddenham, not far from Ely. He sought an explanation for them, from people who knew about the Fens, but as little sensible was suggested, he soon came to the correct conclusion that they were in fact prehistoric barrows. This was an extraordinary discovery.

In England, barrows came in two main varieties: round (mainly Bronze Age) and long (Neolithic). The trouble is, that with the promise of buried grave goods, not to mention treasure, inquiring minds have always been interested in barrows. In the not-too-distant, Victorian past people were perfectly prepared to satisfy their curiosity with a spade. In the last century barrow 'opening' was a respectable occupation for churchmen and the gentry, who might often be found on a summer's afternoon looking on while workmen dug into some unfortunate mound. In such instances each mound took a day or two to excavate, or loot, but seldom any longer. Nowadays an archaeologist would expect to spend six or more weeks excavating a barrow.

Most parts of England, where barrows were still clearly upstanding, were ravaged by Victorian and Edwardian antiquarians. Few places were too remote, be they the Marlborough Downs, the Yorkshire Wolds or the Derbyshire Peaks. Sadly it is hard to think of a single area where the main barrow fields, or cemeteries, remain intact; sadly, too, the records left by the antiquarians are often lacking or woefully inadequate; in many cases the 'records' are simply the hand-written labels on the urns and other items that came from the ground.

So the real importance of David Hall's discovery is that whole barrow fields are now emerging, as the peaty soils 'shrink' away. As the peaty soils 'shrink' they dry out and as they dry out so everything around them, including the barrow and its contents, dries too. So what are we to do? We cannot in all conscience dig the lot, or we will be little better than our antiquarian predecessors. On the other hand, if we do nothing the all-important organic contents of the barrows (for example coffins, leather and fabrics) will dry up and vanish into dust. In my opinion the best-preserved barrow fields, especially those around Haddenham, should be bought for the nation and then kept wet. A few Fenland barrow fields still remain wet, or damp, but others have been drained, almost beyond recall – and quite recently.

The large barrow field of Borough Fen, about 1.6km (1 mile) north-east of Peterborough was still largely waterlogged in the early 1970s, but was deeply drained at the end of the decade. Today the barrows of Borough Fen appear to thrust ever higher through dry peats, and in one or two places their mounds have been cut through by drainage dykes, where we have been able to examine them more closely – and have revealed them to be dry. It is sad to think that these monuments to our Bronze Age and Neolithic ancestors had survived largely intact for 4,000 years, only to be effectively destroyed a couple of years before their significance was recognised. But to be realistic, even if their true importance had been recognised in time, the words of a few archaeologists would have had little effect on the actions of drainage authorities who had the backing of many powerful government agencies, such as the then Ministry of Agriculture. That Ministry had the task of implementing the notorious EEC Common Agricultural Policy that was set up to provide cheap food, at whatever cost to the historic environment, which in this instance amounted to little less than obliteration. The mindless over-drainage of the Fens in the 1970s and '80s still makes me seethe with fury.

Archaeologists have long been fascinated by barrows. They often dominate the skyline and their brooding presence, with its all-encompassing aura of Death, cannot fail to fire the imagination. But most ordinary Bronze Age people were buried closer to home, in the fields and farms where they lived; the barrows were probably reserved for the upper, or elite, classes. We found the graves of several 'ordinary' Bronze Age people at Fengate; some, like the young woman illustrated (*colour plate 10*) were simply laid out along the bottom of a ditch. Was this unceremonial 'dumping', or was it something more subtle? I don't myself believe that people have ever treated corpses as rubbish and I believe the position of the young woman's skeleton in the filling of an important droveway ditch was making a point, probably to do with family or tribal rights to land. But I shall have more to say about this later.

LIFE AND DEATH IN THE BRONZE AGE

So far this chapter has been concerned with the earlier Bronze Age, very approximately the years between 2500 and 1500 BC, and it will shortly be time to move the story on. But, before we do, we should pause and reflect on what it would have been like to have lived in or near the Fens 4,000 years ago. Like any other archaeologist, I have no monopoly on truth. My view of the past is just that: something personal, and sometimes I wonder whether what I can see now in my mind's eye would bear any resemblance at all to the reality of life 4,000 years ago. But having acknowledged that, I still have nothing else to go by. So this, in a nutshell, is how I imagine life was like on the edges of the Fens in the earlier Bronze Age.

As we have seen, during the Neolithic period, society was essentially mobile and had many points in common with the previous world of the hunter and gatherer. Then the population of the region began to grow and the separated clearings in the forests gradually expanded, coming together to form larger tracts of open countryside. At Fengate we now have slight evidence to suggest that the clearing of the trees may initially have been along the lines of traditional roads and migratory routes. Maybe there was a non-functional element to this activity as well. I have often thought that the clearance of the primeval forests was more than just a way of obtaining more farmland – although that must have been a major, probably *the* major consideration.

But there must also have been other factors in people's minds, such as the clearance of sightlines towards features in the landscape that people considered important, such as clefts in hills on the skyline, and so forth. There is now a growing body of evidence to suggest that ideology (including such things as solar and lunar alignments) played a significant role in the laying-out of the earliest landscapes. I have absolutely no evidence to back me up, but I have also felt that the clearance of trees may have become an end in itself. In other words, they *could* do it, so they *did* do it – which is something we may be witnessing in parts of Indonesia and Amazonia today. We should also bear in mind that clearance was a way of establishing a claim to land and it could have been this, rather than the need simply to grow food, that provided the driving force behind the opening-up of the landscape, which in the Fengate area seems to have been well on the way to completion by 3000 BC.

It was at about or shortly after this time that we find a series of barrows or ring-ditches being constructed every 200m or so along the edge of the developing fen at Fengate. These shrines or monuments then became the focus or marker for the laying out of the earliest field system. This later system was itself subdivided into roughly 200m-wide strips by a series of droveways, which were aligned on these ritual or religious monuments. We see something very similar happening just north of Peterborough at West Deeping in the Welland valley – and also further south in the lower Great Ouse valley. So the religious sites, many of which continued in use well into the life of the later field system they helped to mark out, provided the framework for the subsequent landscape. Presumably they served a broadly similar practical purpose in the more open, unenclosed landscapes of the later Neolithic.

The Bronze Age landscape was arranged along the fen-edge and it was divided, as we have seen, every 200m or so by a series of ditched droveways, which radiated out from the wetlands at right-angles. So far as we know there were no villages, or nucleated settlements, to use a convenient jargon term. People chose to live in dispersed farmsteads, with a few outbuildings, which were dotted hither and thither among the ditched droves and paddocks.

The Bronze Age way of life depended to a large extent on livestock, but the rich resources of the Fen nearby were doubtless fully exploited too. We have re-introduced prehistoric livestock to our archaeological park at Flag Fen. This is something of a self-indulgence, as I enjoy working with animals. It gave me

31 Above: A Soay ewe. These are the most primitive breed of sheep in Britain. They survived as a feral population in the Western Isles of Scotland and became fashionable as ornamental park animals in the eighteenth and nineteenth centuries. Closely similar sheep would have grazed the pastures around Flag Fen between 4200 and 1000 BC

32 Opposite above: An elderly 'Iron Age' sow. 'Iron Age' pigs are crosses between wild boar and Tamworths. Tamworths are an ancient breed with characteristically long snouts. The shorter snub snout was bred into pigs from the eighteenth century and results from crosses with oriental breeds

33 Opposite below: An 'Iron Age' sow suckles her litter of eight piglets. The piglets loose their pale stripes after a few months

great pleasure to discover that primitive sheep, such as the Soay breed (*31*), could in fact be worked with dogs – which was something that nobody accepted. I cannot think why, because all sheep are flock animals and they respond to dogs by 'clumping-up' and forming self-protective groups. Pigs, for example, don't behave like this at all and Heaven help any dog that decides to confront a boar! Our pigs were crosses between wild boar and Tamworths (*32*). They look exactly like the long-snouted pigs seen on Iron Age coins. Their stripy piglets are enchanting (*33*). I can imagine that herds of cattle might well have been led out into the Fen in dry summers to exploit the common grazing, just as happened in the Middle Ages. I also suspect that each group of people had a clear idea of where and when they could and could not graze their animals when out in the open Fen. It may have looked open, but in reality it would have been parcelled up and bounded by numerous unwritten laws.

Twenty-five years ago, when I published the Third Fengate Report, which was almost entirely devoted to the Bronze Age field and drove system, I wrote that the dispersed pattern of settlements, taken with other factors such as the regular partition of the land, suggested that society was relatively egalitarian. There were no obvious signs of chiefs, princes or hereditary leaders. If it was not egalitarian and leaderless, which seems improbable, then its component families were fairly independent and did not support a large elite ruling class. I still stand by that.

Anyone who attempts to reconstruct life in the past, and only selects mundane evidence for the humdrum ordinary and 'bog standard', fails to realise that life has always, even in the Bronze Age, been about more than such things. I do not think that we will have significantly advanced our understanding of the past, if the best we can do is picture a Bronze Age farmer driving his cattle to Fen pastures along a hedged drove, having just eaten his breakfast of porridge from an unglazed handmade bowl in a round-house roofed with turf. This surely is just a lifeless description, devoid of any human feeling. It's little better than a specification drawn up for a television set builder. Surely as archaeologists we can do better than this to animate the Bronze Age?

So let us imagine our farmer trudging along the drove. Was he contentedly building up his own family farm, secure in the knowledge that it would pass onto his children, or was he driving his lord and master's animals – with huge resentment? In either case, mere surroundings pale into insignificance; what matters is the motive behind the action. If we are to understand something as cerebral as motive then we must move away from the domestic or agricultural sphere and turn instead to the realms of aspiration and ideology.

In social terms the earlier Bronze Age was essentially a development of the later Neolithic. So far as we can tell, society became less mobile and people settled down within their appropriate tribal areas. There is evidence to suggest that the tribes, rather like the Scottish clans of today, had long histories, which must have been well known by all their individual members. They treated certain sites, such as henges, stone circles or communal tombs, as symbolic, if not actual, tribal centres. There were tribal burial areas, which we call barrow fields, and doubtless the landscape too was carefully parcelled up by a myriad of small signs and symbols of greater or lesser importance. In a stoneless landscape large trees would probably have been important markers, just as we know them to have been in Saxon times.

In some parts of England, such as Salisbury Plain, the great tribal centres of the Early Bronze Age were built of massive stones; Stonehenge and Avebury are obvious examples. Sites like Stonehenge have an earlier phase which features earthen banks and timber posts. Mike Parker Pearson has suggested that the shift from wood to stone marks an important change in emphasis from the living to the dead. It also marks a general 'hardening' of the landscape, whose structure was becoming ever more fixed and permanent. Around Peterborough convenient stone is not available, so use was made of timber and probably of turf too, but there was no long-lived tradition of 'monumentality', of huge, spectacular and lasting centres, such as the great monuments of Wessex. Instead certain parts of the countryside were considered to be specially important and these 'ritual landscapes', as they have been termed, were liberally scattered with hundreds of smaller Bronze Age sites, such as barrows, 'henges' and numerous small family-type shrines, none of which was in use continuously or any length of time, although most show evidence for intermittent use over, perhaps, a generation or two.

The tradition of 'monumentality' never developed in lowland eastern England and it would be a mistake to think of local Neolithic and Bronze Age ceremonial sites as if they were Stonehenge-like churches in which ceremonies took place. Instead, the evidence indicates that the construction and repeated reconstruction of the site was both the end and the means to it: the ceremony was the construction of the place in which the ceremonies took place. In other words, the construction and modification of the monument *was* its use. Incidentally, there is now growing evidence from sites in Wessex, such as the Sanctuary at Avebury that a similar pattern of constructional work for its own sake may have applied in certain instances there too.

I do not think that these ritual sites were necessarily finished or completed in a way that we would recognise today. Instead they were capped-off or 'put to bed' when their period of use came to an end. One henge site excavated by our team in the Welland valley, just north of Peterborough was rebuilt several times and the final phase consisted of a continuous ring-ditch around the outside. There was no entranceway into the interior. The shrine had ceased to be used and had been consigned to another world or dimension, which I would suggest was most probably the world of the Ancestors.

We excavated a number of these Late Neolithic and early Bronze Age religious and ceremonial sites of the Maxey 'ritual landscape' between 1979 and 1986. This landscape lay in the flat, open countryside at the point where the broad lower Welland valley meets the plain around the edge of the Fen. The earliest site, which seems to have been the focus for the subsequent development of the ritual landscape was a causewayed enclosure at Etton. This is neither the place to describe causewayed enclosures, nor that particular site, which I have discussed at length in a recent report, but they were the first major field monuments and began to be constructed around 4000 BC. They seemed to have served a mainly ritual or ceremonial purpose, but that is not to say that they may not also have acted as a focus for settlement, too. The main problem is that, as we have seen, the evidence for earlier Neolithic occupation in lowland England is very hard to pin down. My own feeling is that causewayed enclosures were seasonal meeting places and were probably located on marginal land (for example at the extreme edge of the fen) at the boundaries of tribal territories, or near traditional migratory routes. If the latter is indeed the case, then could one be lurking somewhere in Fengate or Flag Fen, hidden beneath thick deposits of peat and alluvium?

In the original version of this book I suggested that, unless it lies destroyed beneath modern Peterborough, the original ceremonial tribal centre for communities living at Fengate in the Late Neolithic and Early Bronze Age was in the area just discussed, around the little village of Maxey, just north of the modern city. In actual fact Etton is part of a remarkable group of as many as seven causewayed enclosures which I think were positioned at the edge of a major cultural and tribal boundary. North of the Welland causewayed enclosures are absent. So it would not surprise me if the group of seven that we know survive today, may not originally have been rather larger. There are very slight hints indeed that a causewayed enclosure, or some similar type of earlier Neolithic ceremonial site, may lie beneath peat close to the power station at Fengate. The evidence consists of some earlier Neolithic blade-like flints and two fragments of polished stone axes. The stone for these axes came from Langdale in the Lake District and many were found at Etton. More significantly many of the polished axe fragments from Etton appear to have been deliberately broken in a way that detached large flakes of stone. The two fragments from the power station sub-site had been broken in this deliberate fashion.

If a hidden causewayed enclosure might lie at the origins of Neolithic Fengate, what happened at the end of the Early Bronze Age when many of the earlier ceremonial sites went out of use? In the Middle Bronze Age people stopped using barrows to mark the final resting places of their ancestors; henges went out of use and we see new patterns of commemoration and ceremonial assembly emerging, all over Britain. In purely local terms we see the centre of ceremonial activity shift from the Welland valley to the north of the city, across to its eastern Fen fringe. Maybe this reflected changing population dynamics, because we know that the Fengate landscape was becoming more intensively farmed as the Bronze Age progressed. This change from north to east coincided with conditions becoming gradually wetter.

It would be convenient if the changes taking place at the start of the Middle Bronze Age could be linked to a single outside event, such as a massive meteorite impact or a major volcanic eruption. But such things don't happen in tranquil eastern England; and, besides, I am highly suspicious of any explanation for social change that involves a single cause. Human behaviour is more complex than that. So we must seek our agent of change closer to home. In the later Neolithic there is some evidence to suggest that in Wessex, if not elsewhere, society was becoming stratified and there may well have been elite classes of people who did little else but maintain their own authority, through religious observances, lavish funerary rituals and so forth.

It is difficult to be certain, but the general run of evidence from East Anglia points to a rather different tradition, which is why I still stand by my original interpretation of the society behind the Fengate ditched fields as being basically egalitarian. Of course, there must have been a degree of social stratification in earlier Bronze Age societies in the Peterborough region, but I do not believe it was either so pronounced or as well established as in Wessex. Neither the barrows, the 'henges' nor the rich burials of East Anglia are even remotely comparable with their grand contemporaries in Wessex. But that is not to say that East Anglia was economically impoverished – indeed, quite the contrary – it is just that society was organised rather differently.

There can be little doubt that the population around the edges of the Fens was growing throughout the second and third millennia BC. We see evidence for this in the dividing and subdividing of the Fengate Bronze Age landscape. The practice of barrow burial went out of widespread use after about 1400 BC, but it was a very gradual process. It's also worth recalling that barrows had not been used by all classes of society. It was only a small elite that received this treatment when they died; ordinary folk had always been buried less formally. Precisely what replaced barrow burial for the upper echelons has been a moot point in archaeology. Personally I am in no doubt that the bodies of the more privileged members of society were disposed of in a variety of ways; each funeral would have been accompanied by appropriate ceremonial. In some cases the method of disposal would be by cremation; indeed, a Bronze Age cremation cemetery and the remains of a large funeral pyre had been found by Wyman Abbott at Fengate before the Second World War. Another method involved exposure of the body to the crows on platforms (a rather grisly process known as excarnation). Once the physical bodies had been disposed of, the person's life and spirit were then celebrated, perhaps when people came together at the regular, probably annual, gathering.

In the Middle Bronze Age and later, barrow burial was quite perfunctory. Usually it just consisted of a few cremations in urns that were set into the edges of earlier barrows. There also there seems to have been less emphasis on the elaborate or public disposal of the body. The impression one gets is that funerals became smaller in scale – perhaps rather more private, family affairs than major communal gatherings. As the population grew and competition for social prestige rose with it, people wanted to display their wealth and status not only at death, but also in life, when they needed to impress others and make what were, in effect, political statements. This is what we are beginning to see happen between 1500 and 1300 BC when we find the first fine metalwork being deliberately thrown into the waters of rivers and fens.

But there must have been more to it than that. It wasn't all grand items, like swords and daggers that were being offered to the waters. Much of the metalwork at Fengate and Flag Fen was small and insignificant: pins, brooches and razors. These are hardly major symbols of rank and power, so what lies behind their deposition? I shall attempt to answer some of these questions in the next chapter, but for now it is worth noting that the range of metalwork and other items found in the water suggests that a variety of rites took place and that we are not just talking about death.

I would suggest that in the Flag Fen basin area, if not elsewhere, the far-reaching social changes of the Bronze Age were internally generated: the field and drove system continued in use without modification and when it finally started to be abandoned, around 1000 BC, the ceremonial focus that followed it – a massive row of posts – still respected the same orientation of the landscape. This does not seem to me to be evidence for the imposition of new 'Celtic' ideas from outside.

So to summarise, the evidence suggests that influence in the Neolithic and earlier Bronze Age social authority was communal and largely self-imposed. There is little evidence for a powerful elite, as one finds in the rich barrow burials, such as Bush Barrow, in Wessex. As time passed and the population gradually increased we begin to see more clear evidence for social competition. There was then a period, approximately coinciding with the Early Bronze Age, between about 2500 and 1300 BC, of stability, more rapid population growth and social development, that culminated around 1000 BC in changes of far-reaching consequence. These changes involved a new pattern of settlement in which people lived more closely with one another in what were, in effect, embryonic villages.

So, to return to our original question, what was running through the farmer's mind as he drove his animals down the drove? It depends, of course, on precisely when he drove them, but I suspect that earlier in the Bronze Age he would have been more contented with his lot. He would have known where he stood in every sense of the term. Latterly, perhaps after 1500 BC, I imagine he would have worried more about some competing 'upstart' who was disturbing the even tenor of his otherwise tranquil life. He may also have been concerned with cattle rustling and other signs of competition among neighbouring communities. But in both the earlier and the later Bronze Age he would have been prosperous and, so far as we can tell, happy enough. Life may have been short, but I can find no reason to suppose it was either nasty or brutish.

5

The later Bronze Age (1500–700 BC)

The extraordinary timber-built structures at Flag Fen were, in effect, discovered twice: first, in 1982 (the Flag Fen platform) and 1989 (the Fengate power station alignment of posts). We now realise that both sites are part of the same complex, but for present purposes it would be simpler if we considered the two discoveries separately.

THE DISCOVERY OF DEEPLY BURIED SITES

Like many important archaeological discoveries, Flag Fen was found through a combination of luck and opportunism. I am still not entirely sure I believe in archaeological luck. In my opinion lucky archaeologists are people who are prepared to spend time and effort finding nothing. The 'luck' happens when something fills that void. In the case of Flag Fen, it is true that we happened upon a huge timber structure, but nobody hears about the miles of empty dykes we had to walk along before we made that big discovery.

Towards the end of chapter 2, I described how and why we decided to look along freshly machine-cleaned drainage dykes. Put briefly I wanted to find waterlogged sites while they were still wet, and far below the surface; I did not want to find their dried-up remnants blowing around on the surface of an over-drained agri-desert. The idea appealed to English Heritage and they agreed to fund a first season of our new Dyke Survey, starting in the autumn of 1982.

Surveying drainage dykes is very hard work. It involves carrying all sorts of equipment (camera and lenses, surveyor's level, tripod and levelling staff, two range poles, sample bags, finds bags, spade, trowels, notebooks and food for the day), often over very long distances and through heavy clay fields. Much of the time is spent walking awkwardly along the dykeside, at an angle of 45°. It can be a painful process: ankles begin to creak and clay builds-up on boots to give an effect Charles French labelled 'moonboots'.

Sometimes the dykesides are simple to interpret and may consist of just one, single, thick deposit of marine silt. In other cases they can be very complex and require much head-scratching to sort out. The most exciting dykes reveal buried Fen islands whose whole existence was previously unsuspected. In these cases we frequently find evidence that prehistoric groups lived around their fringes, just above the water level.

We began work by walking along dykes to the east of Peterborough, around the village of Eye. The landscape was flat and highly drained and we found little of immediate archaeological interest, other than huge areas of buried and preserved ancient topsoil. This may not sound particularly exciting, but preserved ancient topsoils are very highly valued as sources of information on past environments. Indeed, soil science is one of archaeology's major allies: if I were to be placed on a desert island, with instructions to work out its past, a soil scientist with archaeological experience would be indispensable.

Any archaeologist working in Fenland must have a working knowledge of soils and their recognition, but there are many occasions when more is required, and in such situations I would call on the services of Charles French, our resident archaeological soil scientist, who worked with me throughout the main Fengate and Flag Fen projects. Today he is in the Department of Archaeology at Cambridge. Our association started in 1974, when I was directing the Fengate project, ultimately from Toronto. In those early days I was still building up my team, when a young Canadian approached me for work. He had just gained a degree in archaeology from Cardiff and had a strong interest in archaeological soil science. I could not believe my luck. We worked together at Fengate with great success and Charly decided, with the full backing of friends and colleagues, to go for a post-graduate degree at the Institute of Archaeology (now part of University College) in London. After a brief return to Canada to pick up additional scientific qualifications, he started his research in London while still working for the Fengate project in Peterborough.

His initial work was on the soils that filled Bronze and Iron Age field ditches in Fengate and he was able to plot the process of increasing wetness by analysing the species composition of snails within the ancient soils. Snails and other molluscs are often very fussy about where they choose to live and it is possible to reconstruct the habitats of ancient, long-dead, molluscs if one has detailed knowledge about the residential requirements of their modern counterparts. At least that is the theory. In practice it is much more complex.

Snail shells, especially those of the smaller species, do not survive long in the soil if it is at all acid, and that is a big disadvantage of the technique. On the other hand, pollen rarely survives in chalky, non-acid soils. This means one can analyse molluscs in situations where one cannot examine pollen. Fengate was just such a situation: away from the fen margins it was too dry and alkaline to allow the preservation of pollen, but snail shells survived well.

As Charly's research progressed, he soon realised that snails on their own were not enough, so he broadened his scope to include an even more daunting, but hugely informative approach, known as soil micromorphology. This technique relies on the fact that, when viewed under a microscope, soil particles can reveal their history. This applies not just to their composition (in other words, what they are chemically and physically), but also to the way they sit, or are arranged, in the soil. The analysis begins with a brick-sized block of soil, which is then impregnated with a hard resin. Next it is cut it into thin slices, which are ground down so thinly that they become translucent. These slides are then examined under a powerful microscope, using polarised light.

Soil micromorphology can detect episodes of flooding, forest clearance, permanent pasture, ploughing and burning. It also tells one when a soil has been truncated, for example by turf-cutting or water erosion. Indeed, we have been able to demonstrate turf-cutting in buried soils below barrow mounds some 5,000 years ago.

In most instances archaeological soil scientists are only able to work on ancient soils, or palaeosols to give them their scientific name, in those rare instances where they have been preserved beneath something else on the surface, such as a barrow mound or hillfort rampart. In fact I have heard the excavation of an otherwise unthreatened barrow being justified simply because it would allow soil scientists to sample an intact palaeosol. I'm not sure I altogether approve of that, but in the Fens the situation is very different.

Since the Dyke Survey started in 1982, we have demonstrated that there are thousands of acres of buried ancient soil out there in the Fens, but in these instances the burial leading to preservation was done by the sea or rivers, and not by man. Although less spectacular than the Flag Fen timbers, I would rate this discovery as of equal, or even greater, archaeological significance. Study of these huge tracts of palaeosol will give us important new information on the relationship of people to their changing environment, throughout later prehistory. Such a study will take time and money, but it will be well worth it.

THE DISCOVERY OF FLAG FEN

The discovery of the buried soils in the fens around Eye focused our attention on buried soils, and we became rather good at spotting them – so much so, in fact, that we were in danger of becoming blind to other things. The Dyke Survey operated by finding out in advance from the various drainage authorities precisely where and when they were planning to dredge or enlarge dykes. We could then select which ones to survey. But the early 1980s were still years of agricultural prosperity and many farmers chose to enlarge their own dykes themselves, and these were best spotted from a Land Rover which I drove around speculatively, craning my neck from side to side, on the off-chance I'd spot something interesting. I must have been a danger to the few other motorists on those lonely Fen roads!

One day I was turning off the River Nene embankment near Northey when, looking across the drained peaty 'bay' towards Fengate, I saw the jib of a dragline (a crane-like mechanical digger) in the middle of Flag Fen. I had done my homework with the drainage authorities, I thought, very thoroughly, and I was therefore surprised to see a large digger in a spot I had always been interested in. It clearly wasn't a farmer's machine, as it was far too big. The next day I found an excuse to trudge the short distance along the dyke to the digger and asked the driver who he was working for. It turned out that the particular dyke he was cleaning out belonged to the sewage division of the then Anglian Water Authority, who were based at the picturesquely named Crabmarsh in Wisbech.

The gentleman in charge at Crabmarsh, Mr Beel, was extremely helpful and told us we could do whatever we liked, provided we did not impede the flow of the dyke and risk flooding eastern Peterborough. For the next two weeks we worked along the freshly cleaned dykeside behind the big Anglian Water digger and found a variety of relatively minor archaeological excitements, including more and more buried soil.

At about halfway along its course, we knew that the dyke cut through a Roman road, the Fen Causeway, which ran from the town of *Durobrivae*, just west of Peterborough, to Fengate, Whittlesey and March, eventually joining the East Anglian road system at Denver on the Norfolk fen-edge. I had excavated a trench across the Fen Causeway at Fengate in 1974, but that was on dry land and I was now keen to see how the Roman military engineers had tackled the wetlands proper.

So when our survey encountered the road we slowed right down and began to examine the dyke sides with minute care. Drainage maps show the dyke as the 'Padholme Engine Drain'. An 'engine drain' in Fen terminology is a dyke leading to a pumping engine – in this case three massive pumps housed within the Padholme Pumping Station. These electric pumps lift water from the Engine Drain into the River Nene which flows high above the pumping station behind huge earthen banks.

Being awkward archaeologists we decided to use the dyke's medieval name of 'Mustdyke', which sounds more romantic than the rather utilitarian Padholme Engine Drain in our souvenir guidebooks at Flag Fen. Personally I rather prefer the more modern name. Anyhow, the dragline was digging out the bottom of the dyke, but the sides were barely touched; in some respects this was worse than useless, as the grass was scuffed by the bucket and great gobbets of slimy muck made the going somewhat hazardous. So we had to clean up the section across the Roman road with spades, if we were to see anything at all. This process took at least a day.

The following day we drew and photographed what we had exposed and the day after that we put the finishing touches to the drawings. By now (it was

November 1982) the weather of late autumn was cold and raw, so I decided to pack up and take an early lunch in the warmth of the Dog in a Doublet pub a couple of miles away (and the point where the Nene still ceases to be tidal). I was walking along the top of the dyke, thinking luchtime thoughts, when my foot caught against a piece of wood, which almost tripped me up, and into the slime. Once I had recovered my composure I was surprised at what had happened. It was unheard-of to trip on logs for the simple reason that there were no trees in Flag Fen. Even ancient preserved 'bog oak' was rare here.

So I pulled the wood out of the mud and was even more surprised to see that it had been split across the grain tangentially. This rather unusual type of split is crucially important to our story. But its explanation, will involve the introduction of the second key member of our team, Maisie Taylor.

Had I stumbled on that piece of wood six months previously I doubt whether I would have recognised its significance. The reason for this is that archaeology was (and still is at many universities) traditionally taught as a dryland subject: students learn about bronzes, pottery, animal and human bones, flint and stone tools – all things that survive in dry conditions – but too rarely about timber or woodworking. I had picked up a certain amount of woodworking knowledge by trawling the academic literature, but there is never any substitute for hands-on experience. Like many students I had made pots and knapped flints, but I had never handled ancient or modern timber, other than to assemble the occasional bookcase. So I decided to do something about it.

In 1976 I employed a student at Fengate who was then doing her degree, like Charly, at the Institute of Archaeology in London. While reading for her degree Maisie had developed an interest in prehistoric woodworking and had managed to find courses in wood identification. So she asked me whether I had any ancient timber that needed looking at. As it happened, we had just discovered an early Iron Age well at Fengate, which contained a small oak stake with a carefully cut dovetail joint. This fired Maisie's enthusiasm, but sadly I had little else for her to look at, other than a few rather scrappy flecks of charcoal.

As we didn't have much wood to interest her at Fengate, Maisie turned her attention to Holland where there are many waterlogged sites, rich in timber. At the time she was part of our team, but she would regularly travel to Amsterdam to work on a site at Assendelft that was then being excavated by the Institute of Prehistory there. One day in the autumn of 1982 I persuaded her that she needed an assistant to do things like heavy lifting. Many of the Assendelft timbers were in fact heavy baulks of oak, so I was actually quite useful; as we worked she taught me how to identify the various types of splitting. I should mention here that the reason why people always seemed to be splitting wood in the Bronze Age was quite simply that they did not yet possess effective saws. Bronze axes were used to cut across the grain, but trees were divided along their length by splitting, using wooden wedges.

We have done a certain amount of experimental woodworking at Flag Fen and were taught to do this by Richard Darrah who has an immense amount of practical and theoretical experience of ancient woodworking We could not possibly have managed without his enthusiastic help and never-ending patience.

There are two principal ways of splitting a tree, but both methods require the trunk initially to be split in half. When we first did this I did not believe that Richard would be able to knock his thin, wooden wedges into a felled oak tree, without first cutting a small slot (34). He first removed the bark and then, very gently, started to tap his wedge home. As the harder, seasoned, oak of the wedge bit into the softer, freshly-felled 'green' oak, it began to penetrate, at first slowly, then with greater rapidity. We then hammered wedges in from both sides and within an hour or so we had split our first oak tree trunk in half.

Having split a tree in half, the next stage is to split the half into quarters and then the quarters into eighths and so on, until one has achieved the size required. This, known as a radial split, is by far the easiest type to do, but the resulting timbers are necessarily wedge-shaped, so it is often quite wasteful of wood, as the narrow portion is often removed and discarded (35).

Parallel-sided planks are far less wasteful of timber and can be produced by splitting across the grain, tangentially (*colour plate 11*). It is a far more difficult process than radial splitting and the trick is to place small, sharp, seasoned oak wedges with very great precision in the end-grain (not the sides) and to work only with the very best, straight-grained timber. Even then it takes much skill and good luck to achieve a successful result, particularly when one is working in the middle of a forest, miles from anywhere and on a tree that has fallen into a thick layer of soil and leaf-mould that has half buried the trunk.

This experience of wood and woodworking stood me in good stead as I stood on the brink of the Mustdyke on a cold November day, with a piece of muddy wood in my hands. I was able to recognise that the piece of wood had been split across the grain, tangentially. This way of splitting, rather than sawing suggested quite strongly that the timber was more ancient than modern.

Next I slithered down the side of the dyke to see if I could spot where it had been dredged from by the digger. As I slid down the dykeside, I caught my foot against a small vertical post that protruded through the grass a few feet above the water. The little post was easily pulled from the ground and I was able to identify it as oak (not, I should add, a particularly difficult feat). I was immediately struck by the fact that the post was quite dry and weighed almost nothing, yet oak is usually very dense. I was also struck by the fact that the tip had been sharpened all round, pencil-fashion, by an axe with a very narrow, curved blade – no more than about 40mm (1.5in) wide. Today many Fen dykes have posts in their sides to reinforce areas of loose peat or of 'running silts' (old stream courses that are still partially active). I knew, however, that this particular dyke was fairly stable, and besides, modern posts are usually of pine or spruce, chemically treated, and invariably saw-sharpened.

So I hung my coat on a ranging pole that I had driven into the ground to mark the precise spot where I had found the post and started to chop into the

34 Splitting a freshly felled oak tree trunk in half, using wooden wedges. The wedges are made from hard, seasoned oak and can be tapped into the soft outer sapwood of the tree without making a slot, once the bark has been removed. Bronze Age carpentry depended on split timber because efficient saws had not yet been invented

35 Wedge-shaped radially split oak planks. The centre and left hand planks had been split with steel wedges which have bruised the wood and left dark marks (the reaction of iron and tannic acid in the oak). The plank to the right was split with wooden wedges and no marks are visible

dykeside with my trowel. No sooner had I started to clear the grass than I found small pieces of wood protruding from the dykeside, slightly less than 1m (3ft) above the post. There was something about the regularity of their arrangement that made me think that they had been put there by the hand of man, perhaps as part of a track or something of the sort. Then I happened to look up, along the dykeside, back towards the Roman road whose orange gravel seemed to glow in the distance. I still recall the shiver I felt when I suddenly realised that the pieces of wood I had exposed with my trowel lay about 1m (3ft) *below* the bottom of the Roman road.

If one assumes that the peats thereabouts had accumulated at the rate of about 1mm (0.04in) a year, then there was every chance that the post and the smaller timbers dated to about 1000 BC – roughly a millennium before the road, which was most probably constructed just after the mid-first century AD. I then retrieved a camera from my coat pocket and recorded the scene for posterity. That view only survives as colour plate 3 in the 1991 edition of this book. Sadly the original slide was destroyed, along with several thousand others in my collection, in the Flag Fen fire of January 2000. The loss of this particular slide felt a bit like the loss of an old friend.

After a quick and very late lunch I very reluctantly decided not to return to the dyke, as conditions were deteriorating rapidly. The light was failing, and freezing fog was rolling in from the Wash. So I drove home, tired but happy. We could not get back to the dyke for a couple of days, the weather being so bad, but when eventually we did, it was with a team of six people. I had described what I had found and we all agreed that it sounded like the remains of a timber trackway, rather like the ones that the Somerset Levels Project were finding at the time. So we returned, and by now we were equipped with spades and other heavy tools – and we were prepared to use them. When we reached the spot where I had left the ranging pole marker I immediately resumed trowelling where I had left off, fully expecting, if it was indeed a trackway, to come across its edges before too long. But strangely I did not; it seemed to be continuing.

Then, and from about 18m (60ft) to my right, Charles French gave a shout and we all rushed over (in a thoroughly unprofessional manner) to see what he had found. At his feet lay a 15cm (6in) wide, tangentially split oak plank with other oak pieces around it. So we enlarged our makeshift excavation on either side of this new find. A few moments later David Gurney (who is now Principal Archaeologist for Norfolk Landscape) found another large split oak plank, but this time it had a mortice hole, through which a peg had been driven. This was particularly important as it provided that the plank and the peg were still *in situ*, precisely where they had been placed in prehistoric times.

Then there was another cry from David Crowther (who went on to do pioneering research along the Humber foreshore). Dave was working an improbable 27m (90ft) away and he had found more planks. I remember standing near the ranging pole and looking around me. I simply couldn't understand what was going on. Dave and Charly, the two people on either side of my original find, were about 36m (120ft) apart. No prehistoric trackway in Somerset, or indeed anywhere else, could have been *that* wide. At the time none of us believed for a moment that we were revealing parts of the same site. Surely this mass of timber had to represent the remains of several structures that had accumulated through time? It seemed like the only logical explanation.

We broke for lunch in a state of great over-excitement, gobbled down our sandwiches and returned to the fray. Everywhere we looked we seemed to find ancient timber. By the end of the day the dykeside looked as if a bomb had hit it. There was wood and peat everywhere. Later in the afternoon, we looked back at the devastation as we started to head home, and we decided it was time we began to behave more like professional archaeologists. Accordingly, the next day we tidied up the loose earth and began to excavate a step-like trench along the dykeside, in the hope that at some point the spread of wood would cease. Although quite dry, because it was so close to the edge of the dyke, some of the wood was still remarkably well preserved and one piece in particular seems to have been used as a carpenter's chopping block as it carried the distinct tool-marks of some six separate implements, mainly axes and chisels.

FLAG FEN: DISCOVERING THE SIZE OF THE SITE

After three days' work it was apparent to all of us that we had discovered something of major importance so I decided to find out who actually owned it. This was something I should have done many months previously, but I can be very lazy about office work and administration. So I left the two Daves and Charles French digging, with Maisie rushing from one to another examining the wood, and headed for Anglian Water in Wisbech. Mr Beel heard my story and then said he had a small confession to make. It would appear that Anglian Water had last deepened and enlarged that dyke in 1976 and he was the Resident Engineer on the job. He remembered the spot well, because their mechanical digger had actually been brought to a standstill by vast amounts of timber, which they had thought – quite reasonably – were the remains of a Victorian sluice. I remember replying that, if that was an example of his artefact-dating, he had better stick to engineering and stay well clear of archaeology!

Despite my abuse, Mr Beel then set about helping us in every way possible. We were given a boat and a secure place to work from, and we learned that the land to one side of the dyke belonged to the Anglian Water Authority (now Anglian Water) who used it for the spreading and disposal of Peterborough's sewage sludge. We had certainly noticed a slight heaviness in the air. I was then put in touch with the Authority's estates people, with whom we negotiated access rights.

Meanwhile, the team in the dyke were still digging away, with no sign of an end in sight. Eventually, after about two weeks' work the wood ceased to appear, but not before we had excavated, planned, photographed and exposed over 80m (260ft) of timber along the dykeside (*36*). Next we had to sample and remove about 500 pieces which were threatened with immediate destruction now that we had exposed them to the air. We did this by boat until, in the second week of December the weather clamped down, and then we used the Anglian Water Authority's tough little double-hulled fibreglass boat as a sledge on the frozen water.

The last pieces of wood were prised from the ground by frozen fingers on Christmas Eve. By this time most of the team had returned to their families for the festivities and I well remember the strange feeling when, as Maisie and I hauled the last boatload of wood along the dyke and it began to snow lightly, we realised that Peterborough had gone silent for the holiday. By nine o'clock the normal roar of traffic had ceased and for a few moments, trudging through the mud in the middle of nowhere, we felt more in touch with the remote past than with our own time. That strange sensation still lingers with me today.

36 The Mustdyke at Flag Fen three weeks after the initial discovery of wood. Timbers can just be seen on the left-hand side of the continuous step or working platform we had dug, half a metre, or so, above the water level. The gravel spread of the Roman road is visible behind and above the far figure

After Christmas we were visited by Dr Geoffrey Wainwright, the senior archaeologist at English Heritage. By this time Flag Fen had received much media attention and I felt somewhat uneasy, as I knew Geoff could be very sceptical and could see through media 'hype'. He was also more than accustomed to the over-enthusiasm of his colleagues. We were both walking along the Mustdyke on a fine January morning and were approaching the site, when suddenly, and without any warning at all, a grass snake slithered out of the mud in front of us. It shimmered down the dykeside and entered the water without a ripple. We were both delighted at this and the mood then became more relaxed and positive. Subsequently I have discovered how much Geoff likes and understands wildlife. Anyhow, I hope that snake lived happily, had a large family – and died of a surfeit of frogs.

As we discussed the site over lunch, Geoff put his finger on our problem: we had over 80m of prehistoric timber, representing a vast amount of labour, and yet we had not found anything else. There were, as yet, no pots, flints or bronzes. Yet it was undoubtedly an important site because why else should they have expended so much time and effort on its construction? Put another way: it was important, but what was it? Geoff was reluctant to commit large sums of money to a site of unknown size or purpose, which, in retrospect, I can now see was reasonable enough, although at the time, of course, I felt we should be given carte blanche to do anything we chose, regardless of expense. Geoff wanted us to adopt a staged approach. A few days later we were told we could spend £4000 to discover (a) what it was and (b) its size. A challenge, I thought – and with some justification.

The following year was frantically busy, but not at Flag Fen. Our main site in 1983 was the partially waterlogged Neolithic causewayed enclosure at Etton, in the Welland valley, just north of Peterborough. The quarry next to this site had turned its huge pumps on and we were digging flat out to recover everything we could before the entire site was sucked dry. It was hard work, but worth it. It produced an extraordinary amount of material, including a wooden Neolithic axe handle and the earliest piece of fine string yet found in England. The string was made from flax and a report on the discovery printed in a newspaper found its way into the 'True Stories' column of *Private Eye*. I was delighted. We also found the earliest dog mess in Britain and that managed to achieve nearly two column-inches in *The Sun* – which was all a bit peculiar.

By the end of the summer we all needed a rest, but instead we started at Flag Fen. At the time I felt it should be renamed Flagging Fen. It had been a very hot season and when we returned to the Mustdyke we were shocked by the state of things. The dyke was almost dry and the few pieces of Bronze Age wood that we didn't manage to remove the previous season were now twisted, cracked and worthless. We could not dig away from the dykeside, as the land there was now occupied by a fine field of standing wheat. So, after looking around, we decided to place a trench on the dykeside in an area of upright posts (37). We had spent

37 The early summer of 1983 had been hot, and when we returned to Flag Fen later in the season we excavated a small trench into the post alignment on the dykeside. We were appalled by the dry state of the timbers, which had become badly split, cracked and distorted

a couple of days digging there, when combine harvesters arrived and the wheat was duly harvested.

Next day the straw and stubble were set alight and we were given three days to complete a borehole survey, before the tractors returned to sow the next season's crop. In those days land in East Anglia did not spend much time lying fallow. Meanwhile, the weather stayed hot and dry. Then the wind got up. Soon it blew a gale. In the gales dry peat was blown off the land surrounding the site and it swiftly fell to earth in the relatively still air of the dyke. Sometimes we would return in the morning to find a thick layer of wind-sorted dry peat covering the wood we had spent the previous day uncovering. It could be quite frustrating and I remember thinking how insane it all was: here we were at a metre above sea level trying to contend with near-desert conditions, when by rights we ought to have been up to our waists in water.

The time available to us was limited so Charly and I rapidly laid out a 20m (66ft) grid over the field surface. Then we started to drill boreholes by hand. It was back-breaking work, especially pulling the drill out against the vacuum caused by damp peat, but it was worth the pain. After three days we had a fairly clear picture: wood, and much of it oak or ash which could not have grown in the peat, and must therefore have been brought in from outside, extended over an area of about 0.8ha (2 acres). The site was far, far larger than we had ever imagined. Then the tractors rolled onto the field and we returned to the dykeside trench amongst the uprights.

We soon found the tops of the first posts, many of which were oak, and we started to work our way down. About 60cm (2ft) below their tops (which had rotted off at some time in the distant past) we came across horizontal timbers. These were removed to reveal smaller pieces, including many woodchips, which strongly suggested that an axe, or axes, had actually been used *in situ*. The woodchips rested in a mixture of peaty mud and a very distinct coarse white sand with fine gravel pebbles which Charles French said could not have been washed there by water, as the stones were too large and heavy. Presumably this gravel had been dumped there in prehistoric times. We also found a plank with a single mortice hole cut through it; sadly it was starting to dry out and was beginning to break up (*38*). This was all very intriguing, but we had still not answered Geoff Wainwright's first, and most important, question: what was it?

About a week into the excavation, Charly French found five pieces of coarse, handmade pottery from the same vessel (*39*). I took one look and was in no doubt

38 An oak plank with a single mortice hole from the area of the post alignment. This plank was found in the 1983 excavations on the edge of the Mustdyke and it is showing clear signs of disintegration as a result of drying out

39 Five pieces of undecorated Late Bronze Age pottery found in the excavations of 1983. The two conjoining sherds had broken in antiquity; the right-hand sherd of the two was part of a simple rim

at all that this pottery was of Middle or Late Bronze Age date. It was too horrible (i.e. coarse and crudely made) to be anything else. Southern English Late Bronze Age pottery is rarely decorated and often seems to have been made by folk who took a delight in doing things badly. The pieces before us were no exception, and had the look and texture of wet wholemeal biscuit. This texture is often caused by the dissolving out of fossil shell originally ground up and added to the clay as a tempering agent; the temper allowed a cooking pot to be repeatedly heated without cracking – a type of prehistoric Pyrex. We will see below that later Bronze Age pottery can sometimes be very fine, but this is the exception, rather than the rule.

A few months previously, the British Museum Research Laboratory had rushed us through a radiocarbon date that placed the dykeside timber in the Late Bronze Age, just after 1000 BC. Those few sherds of pottery were all-important, as they provided independent confirmation of the radiocarbon date. The form of the vessel, which was a simple jar, suggested that it once served a domestic or household purpose. Of course it could have been thrown into Flag Fen from a boat, with the rest of the household rubbish, but the usual practice in pre-Roman Britain was to dump refuse near the spot where it had been produced. It was rarely transported any distance, and as the closest dry land was at least 200m away, it seemed reasonable to suppose that people who used and made the pottery might have lived, or camped, nearby in the wetland.

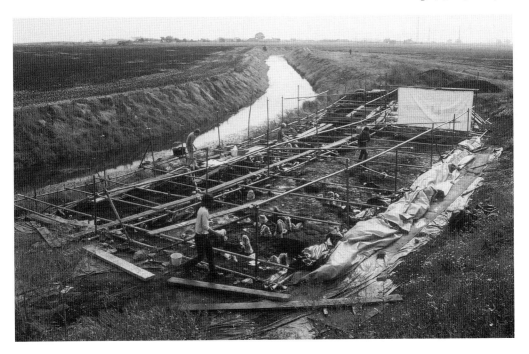

40 The excavations of 1984 and 1985 were along the side of the Mustdyke. This view is looking south-east towards Northey, with the chimneys of the Whittlesey brickworks on the horizon. The scaffolding was used to support tarpaulins and plastic sheeting to shield against the sun

The few finds and other results of the 1983 survey and excavation were sufficiently encouraging for English Heritage to give us a grant for a proper excavation for the next year (1984). By now we had established excellent relations with the water authorities who agreed to retain the dyke water at a higher level in an effort to slow down drying out.

Flag Fen had also been visited by Professor Leendert Louwe-Kooijmans of Leiden University in the Netherlands. Leendert had extensive experience of de-watered peat sites and reckoned that the timbers of Flag Fen would be seriously decayed within 15 to 20 years, unless something was done to slow down desiccation. At the time there was no alternative but to excavate, since the only solution, as we then thought, was to flood the whole of Flag Fen and with it the farms and houses of many of its modern inhabitants. Since then we have constructed the artificial lake and are learning how to provide protection by raising water levels artificially – but more on this later.

In the 1984 season of excavation we decided to enlarge the previous year's small trench around the posts, and then to concentrate our efforts along the edge of the dyke, because that was where drying out was most severe. We were now working on a much bigger scale than hitherto (*40*). When we started work we found that the upper soil had been compacted into an almost solid mass by the heavy machines that had been used to dredge the dyke in 1976 and 1982.

Try as we would, we simply could not shift it by hand. So I decided to call in a machine of our own to clear a reasonably-sized area. Before I opened the trench I determined to carry out a search of the topsoil surface before disturbing it with the digger and with spoil heaps.

We did not expect to find anything very ancient in the topsoil, as the Bronze Age levels were all deeply buried, but in the material that had been dredged out of the dyke we found about half a dozen human bones, which we assumed, for no reason at all, were the remains of medieval fishermen. In 1989 we found another two loose human bones, again alongside the Mustdyke, but on the surface.

After our machine had removed the tough upper crust, we took off the remaining overburden by hand. We placed our trench alongside the dyke and made it just 5m (16ft) wide and 10m (33ft) long, although it grew in length as time progressed. As we came down on the tops of the posts it was quite apparent that they were arranged in four somewhat irregular rows (41). We continued to dig downwards, below the post tops, and about half a metre lower down we encountered the first horizontal wood.

As we noted the previous year, the highest horizontal wood was invariably unsplit ('roundwood' to give its correct name) and was more spread out and

41 Posts of the alignment in 1984. By now the wood along the dykeside was almost fully dried out. Note the coarse sand and fine gravel below the planks in the foreground; this had been brought to Flag Fen as grit for the slippery surfaces of wet planks

less cluttered than the timber below. We left the highest timber in place, as we could work around it, and continued to work our way even further down. The next layer of wood we came to was also rather irregular and consisted mainly of roundwood too, but individual pieces were generally smaller. Below this was the layer of small woodchips and coarse white sand and gravel that we had come across the previous season – in which we had found the five fragments of pottery.

By now we were becoming swamped with wood, so we removed the upper two layers, to expose the layer of chips and sand below them. This layer was very much flatter than the previous two and had a clearly defined surface. We also gained the impression that it was thicker in places where it had been laid over hollows; in many parts there were also clear indications that planks or small boards had been laid down as a support or reinforcement beneath. Rather to our relief we also found more archaeological artefacts in amongst the sand and woodchips: several dozen sherds of coarse Bronze Age pottery, some very crudely fashioned flint implements and a fossil echinoid, or sea urchin, about the size of a tennis ball, which I stoutly maintain (but cannot demonstrate) was a child's toy. The layer of sand, woodchips and pottery was only found within the area occupied by the vertical posts – and was found nowhere else.

Flag Fen was quite unlike any other site we had excavated until that point, and its interpretation was clearly going to cause us difficulties. At first glance one might assume that because we had so much information, and it was all so very well preserved, that understanding its significance would be relatively straightforward. That is not always the case however. In my experience, the more archaeological information you possess, the more (and not the less) there is to explain. Poorly preserved archaeological evidence seems easy to interpret and can be very convincing to everyone – except those who have had to wrestle with well-preserved complex sites themselves. It's rather like the difference between prehistoric and historic archaeology. I have just completed a book on Dark Age Britain and, for the first time in my archaeological career, I have had to face the problems posed by language – in this case the adoption of English. If one takes archaeological evidence alone, then a very good case can be made against Anglo-Saxon mass migration, but when the 'language factor' is added to the mix, certainty becomes impossible – either way.

This 'uncertainty principle' applies to Fengate and Flag Fen. The very first, earlier Neolithic, landscape (chapter 3) is just hinted at by a few aligned ditches and mortuary structures, and yet it is quite convincing. Flag Fen, on the other hand, is superbly preserved, but there are still huge problems that cannot be resolved, because the sheer diversity of evidence is always providing good reasons to refute all simple explanations.

HOW WE EXCAVATED THE FLAG FEN TIMBERS

It was clear that the sand and woodchip layer at Flag Fen was *in situ*. It was also apparent that it was closely associated with the posts, as it did not occur away from them. The posts had all been carefully mapped onto large-scale plans, and it was immediately apparent that they formed four – and maybe five – distinct rows. The rows, moreover, were plainly parallel and this suggested that they ought either to be contemporary with each other, or were part of a single structure that was repaired and renewed over time. After much head-scratching we decided that we were excavating the remains of a rectangular building, of as yet unknown length, constructed on a large timber platform in the middle of the fen.

The width of the hypothetical building, 6m (19ft) was closely comparable with an almost contemporary example at the site of Assendelft in Holland, as were the other dimensions of its three-aisled construction. Moreover, coarse white sand which was often found within the area of the posts at Flag Fen (*colour plate 12*) is frequently found on the floors of houses built on 'crannogs' in Scotland and Ireland. Crannogs are fortified farmsteads built on artificial islands just off the shores of lochs and lakes. The coarse sand was spread to prevent feet sliding about on wood made dangerously slippery with wet peat, algae and general fenny slime. On the dig we used chicken wire as a more durable modern substitute.

The house hypothesis made, and still makes, sense. It just happens to be wrong. It explains the presence of broken household pottery, of animal bones and flint tools. But there are drawbacks, too: principally the plethora of posts, which as we will see below, can now be explained. The upper two layers, above the floor spread with coarse sand, could be explained as collapse from roof and walls.

The following season (1985) we continued in the same trench and were beginning to develop excavation techniques that were suited to a site that had no edges or 'safe' areas where we could kneel and work. First, however, we had to remove the overlying peat and alluvium, which we did by machine until the tops of the first posts were encountered. During the previous season we had boxed, or encased, the trench in scaffolding, which simply rested on the ground, except along the dykeside where it was safe to drive in scaffold poles as support posts. This framework had to break all the accepted rules of scaffolding, but it was low enough to be safe if a collapse did happen. More importantly, it worked; it was stable and was heavy enough to withstand the worst gales of winter which could be very fierce in that flat, treeless landscape.

We used the scaffold framework to divide the trench up into smaller areas and it provided a means of fixing suspended plank platforms above the wood, from which people could work. We found that sunlight and wind rapidly dried the wood, so we stretched light, woven tarpaulin sheets over the scaffold frame as shelter. Sadly, this was never very satisfactory and after windy nights we would often return to find ropes snapped, eyelets ripped out and the sheets in tatters.

In 1984 we kept the timbers wet with relays of watering cans, but this again was not altogether satisfactory, and in 1985 we replaced cans with an aged agricultural sprinkling system which usually worked but which we found less endearing when the ancient tractor's battery failed, or its fuel lines or filters blocked up with air-borne peat.

On our dryland excavations we had often used sieves of various sorts as a means of trying to standardise what we recovered from the ground. In theory (although not, I suspect, in practice) archaeological sieves are meant to remove the bias in finds' distribution caused by sharp-eyed versus myopic excavators. At Flag Fen we found that sieves of all types simply clogged up with wood and peat; we persisted in trying to make use of them until about 1995 when we gave up in disgust. Latterly we have only sieved small samples of soil as a 'control' to see whether we are being grossly incompetent.

In 1986 we acquired a more robust type of industrial shelter from a friendly and helpful firm in Bedford and we used the same firm's large plastic-covered temporary warehouse to shelter the dig. This extraordinary building stood through the 1987 hurricane in southern England and is built in Sweden to their very demanding Building Regulations. It continued in use until our last season of large-scale work in 1995. In the new building we abandoned the system of suspended working platforms and devised a simpler ground-based system using strips of discarded industrial flooring to spread people's weight.

When we started work in 1984 we would draw plans of the wood by balancing on the scaffolding and looking down through a small gridded-frame. This was often rather perilous and not always very accurate. So we made a rather crude photo-montage of the wood using a specially adapted surveyor's level tripod. Charly French was the star planner, using this technique, but after we had acquired the new building we constructed a more sophisticated system, based on a monorail-mounted camera that travels around a U-shaped rail in the roof of the structure. This system was built with help of engineering students at Peterborough Regional College. It produced an accurate photo-montage of each level of timber, which we then traced over to make our working plans. It also provided us with splendid bird's eye views. The several photo-montage plans proved very useful in their own right and have been reproduced in full in the Flag Fen Basin Report, where they look most spectacular.

The winter of 1984/85 was quite severe and we had 'put the site to bed' that autumn beneath a thick layer of straw between two layers of plastic sheeting. In theory it was a splendid idea, and was based on what local farmers did to keep frost off their potato clamps. But when it came to removing the straw we found that the large local population of rats, grown fat on their diet of sewage sludge, had found it an ideal spot to nest over winter and raise healthy young families of ratlets. I need hardly add that we did not repeat the experiment. When the covers were eventually cleared of straw and rodents we found that the archaeological layers had survived unscathed, so we resumed work on the sand and chip floor.

THE 'HOUSE HYPOTHESIS'

We had put forward the building hypothesis, to explain the posts and the sandy 'floor' in 1984 and we now sought evidence to prove or disprove it. The two outer rows of posts were taken to be the walls, and in the north wall there was a clear doorway-sized gap. A certain amount of sand and fine gravel had been spread immediately outside the gap, presumably by trampling feet. As if to confirm the idea that this was indeed a threshold we found a very large tangentially split oak plank with two mortice holes. Another, smaller plank had been jammed between it and the presumed doorpost and a stout peg had been driven through one of the mortice holes, so that it was flush with the surface. Outside this 'doorway' was what we took to be the 'yard' of the platform,

This 'yard' had been additionally consolidated with numerous oak timber off-cuts and a discarded yoke-like object with two perforations (now in The British Museum collections). Only a small part of the 'yard' surface north of the posts was inside the trench, but our excavations in 1985 and 1986 showed it to have been carefully built, with a surface that had been pegged in position in places. One of these pegs had been cut from a coppiced or pollarded tree and given a sharpened tip. The piece at the top was plainly part of the coppice 'bole' and consisted of highly characteristic gnarled, burr wood. In other words, the peg was complete; it could never have extended any higher. When we excavated it, the gnarled top of the peg protruded some 7.5-10cm (3-4in) above the yard surface it had originally held in place. This demonstrated (a) that the yard surface was *in situ* and (b) that shrinkage caused by drying out was not as severe – as we had once feared. Below the 'yard' surface we were amazed to come across not rough brushwood and scrappy off-cuts and rejects, as we had anticipated, but large baulks of trimmed timber, much of it, moreover, of oak.

Our first significant interpretational breakthrough was unexpected. In amongst the lowest, largest timbers we found our first really unusual find: a fragment of polished shale bracelet. On dry sites, ancient shale tends to flake and laminate, but our example was black and glossy. It looked brand new; indeed, I have seen identical bracelets on my grandmother's dressing table. We have since found several more, and although such bracelets are not unusual on Late Bronze Age domestic sites, we were still delighted. Apart from anything else, it tended to support our house hypothesis.

The posts of the 'building's' south wall also featured a doorway-sized gap, but it was not precisely opposite the threshold on the north side. It looked rather odd and asymmetrical on plan, but we reasoned such a staggered arrangement would help to baffle through-draughts. The south wall doorway seemed to have been 'paved' with a thick layer of woodchips, and, again, the yard outside showed signs of trample and surface timbers had been pegged down in many places. The 'doorpost' was a stump with a protruding peg which may originally fitted into a socket in the door. A similar, but reversed arrangement is known from a prehistoric door in Switzerland. The trouble is that Maisie is now convinced, having found other examples of such strange, peg-like protrusions, that this is a product of shrinkage following drying out and probably has much to do with the different densities of heartwood and sapwood. In other words she is certain that this is not a man–made phenomenon.

We next turned our attention to the outside walls of the hypothetical 'house'. The south wall, east of the doorway, was the best preserved, and here we found the very base of the wall which consisted of two planks, one on the inside and one on the outside of the building, which were pegged against the main roof-support posts. These carried the weight of the wall cladding and would be termed by architects a 'sill-plate'. The wall cladding consisted of long rods, about 5cm (2in) in diameter which were pegged against the posts by vertical pegs driven into the peat (42). This gave, in effect, a cavity wall slightly less than 50cm (20in) thick. The surrounding peaty alluvium would have made an excellent 'daub', but it is difficult to say with any confidence whether or not it was used to coat the walls. We will see shortly that we do not now believe that this was a daubed wall, but may have served as a revetment or reinforcement to the causeway formed by the post alignment.

42 When we still believed that the posts of the post alignment were part of a long rectangular building, this arrangement of rods and small timber pegged on either side of the external rows of posts, looked remarkably like a cavity wall. We now believe that this 'wall' was a revetment intended to protect the slightly raised surface of a causeway

Below the floor layer, or layers, the foundations consisted of many large timbers which were clearly intended either to carry a substantial load or else to spread a relatively light load but in extremely soft, boggy ground. We now believe it was the latter. Some of what we then believed were wall and roof support posts had collapsed, and one had come down on a near-complete pot.

Maisie Taylor has identified many samples of wood and has shown that oak was almost invariably split or modified in some way and was most commonly used in and around the post alignment. Ash was a less important building timber, and was frequently split into halves. Rather surprisingly, the types of wood that grow most readily in the fen, namely willow, sallow and poplar, were used infrequently, with the important exception of alder, which is probably the single most commonly found species of tree at Flag Fen. When kept wet alder resists rot well, but is otherwise a poor timber for construction purposes.

Slightly more than 1m (3ft) outside the south 'wall' was a very widely spaced row of posts which leaned away from the 'building'. These were thought to have been used to support broad eaves, needed to keep mud walls dry. Beyond these hypothetical eaves-support posts was the southern platform or 'yard' surface. The south platform area was made up from rather smaller wood than that to the north, but it still included many carpentry off-cuts and a few artefacts, such as a finely made willow scoop.

THE EDGES OF THE PLATFORM

In 1986 we decided to investigate the edge of the platform to the south of the posts, since the dykeside investigation of 1982, had shown it to peter out in a rather unconvincing fashion. So we extended the 5m (16.5ft) wide trench along the dyke and, just as in 1982, the spread of wood kept on going. Eventually it ceased to appear. As we had suspected from the outset, instead of petering out, the platform had been carefully edged with a 'boardwalk' about 3.5m (11ft) wide made from planks and roundwood arranged circumferentially, parallel with the edge of the platform (not, as we had suspected, radially or spoke-fashion) (43). One of the split oak planks was an extraordinary 3.25m (10ft) in length. There were a few isolated pieces of driftwood beyond the 'boardwalk', but these aside, the contrast between the timber platform and the surrounding empty fen was most marked.

The following season (1987) we investigated the foundations of the perimeter 'boardwalk' which had been built upon at least three layers of timber, laid in a rough criss-cross pattern. But perhaps the most interesting discovery came last. The lowest timbers included a very large oak post with a pencil-like sharpened tip. We at once recognised it as an upright that had been pulled from the ground, and there was distinctive yellowy-grey clay still sticking to its tip. This clay had preserved the axe-marks beneath it superbly, and in this particular case the post

43 The artificial timber platform at Flag Fen was edged by a form of boardwalk, composed of planks laid on top of logs. This view shows the planks being excavated in 1985. The remains of a shrub or small tree, which grew on the platform after it ceased to be maintained around 900 BC, can be seen to the right of the scale

had been sharpened by an axe with two deep notches in its blade, which show up clearly as low ridges in the wood. Less than a pace away was the hole from which it had been extracted (by pulling, not digging) before being dropped on the ground. There were no other posts in the immediate vicinity, so it is currently difficult to decide whether this massive post stood on its own, or formed part of an encircling defensive palisade.

The story of the edge revetment was resumed in the spring of 1988 when many of our visitors expressed a wish to see something 'fenny', that resembled Bronze Age Flag Fen. The planting of trees, shrubs and marginal reeds around the lake had yet to grow up, and I decided to make a ramp down to the Mustdyke whose edges were covered with reeds, rushes and sedge; we then planned to build a wooden walkway to the main excavation along the dykeside 'step' (what was left of the 1982 excavations along the dykeside just above the water level); as a bonus, people on their way to the dig could view the Roman road from under a protective shelter. The ramp was positioned to one side of the spread of timber (as revealed in our borehole survey), and well north of the point where it had petered out in our initial excavations along the dykeside, in 1982. Needless to state, despite our careful plans to avoid coming down on any timbers, we placed the ramp right on top of the platform's northern perimeter.

We were at the extreme edge of the dyke and as a consequence drying out was quite severe. Despite this we were able to excavate the trunks of several trees, mainly of alder, which had been placed on the ground in precisely the same way as the more formal perimeter 'boardwalk' at the other side of the platform. Again, the trunks had been raised on a foundation of horizontal timbers, but this was less robustly constructed than that below the other 'boardwalk'.

In 1986 we at last obtained permission to do a borehole survey on the other, east, side of the Mustdyke. This was not made any easier by the presence of the Roman road which ran across the area, but we were able to demonstrate that there was wood extending in a large semi-circle from the two extremes in the dykeside about 40-50m (130-165ft) into the field. This additional survey now gave us a fairly good impression of the hidden timber platform's actual size. In 1987 we constructed the Mere and in the process discovered more evidence for the size of the platform, including posts of at least one other alignment or causeway. In subsequent years we were able to excavate trial trenches which provided us with important pollen and environmental samples and further information about the size and make-up of the platform The environmental samples confirmed that the area around the platform was extremely wet in the Bronze Age, with open water that supported true aquatic plants, such as water lilies. We drew all this information together for a plan of the timber platform which appeared in the Flag Fen Basin Report (44).

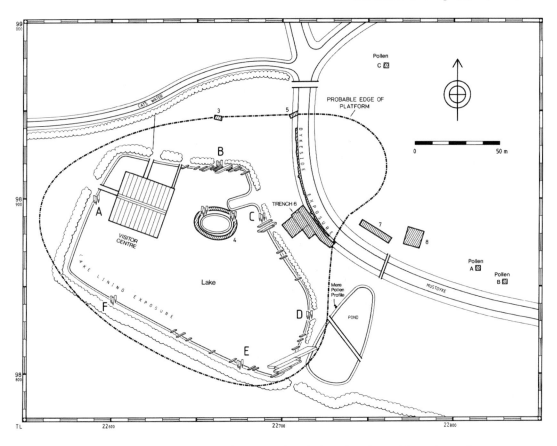

44 Plan of the known extent of the Flag Fen timber platform, based on trial trenches and information gathered during the construction of the lake. The extent of the platform north-east of the Mustdyke was assessed by a borehole survey. The plan also shows the location of pollen sample trenches. *From* The Flag Fen Basin Report, *courtesy of English Heritage*

PUBLIC ARCHAEOLOGY AT FLAG FEN

The year 1987 was crucially important to the development of Flag Fen as a visitor attraction. The previous winter Geoffrey Wainwright had secured us a conditional promise of £475,000 from English Heritage, to be spent over the five years from 1988 to 1992. This sum was subject to strict Treasury limits and could not be 'stretched' by special pleading, which was something I was then quite good at! We were now confronted by a financial 'brick wall' which we know we were bound to hit. But we still had time to make plans. We decided that now was the time to 'go public' so that year (1987) we opened the site for a trial period of 13 weeks from August to October.

I have already mentioned the construction of the lake (chapter 2), and while we were digging down to insert the plastic film, we encountered wood virtually everywhere. This confirmed our fears that the borehole survey had been rather conservative about the extent of the platform. More importantly, we found groups of buried posts at no less than seven different points around the lake's circumference. Of course without excavation we were unable to tell what these posts represented: some may have been buildings, others could have been causeways or palisades. We simply did not know.

It was, however, clear that the public would not be particularly impressed by our dykeside excavations which we had started in 1984 and were by then nearing completion. By this late stage I have to admit that they were beginning to look rather tired and worn out. We needed something new to show people. So as a first step we decided to concentrate our efforts at the northern end of the dykeside trench and remove everything there.

Slightly to our surprise we found that none of the posts in this area had been dug into the ground. Such posts would have had flat bases, which would have rested on the bottom of the post-hole. Instead all the Flag Fen timbers had been given long pencil-like sharpened tips that had then been pile-driven into the clay and gravel that underlies the peat. When the last of these posts had been removed, we erected the new Swedish building that we had found from the firm in Bedford the previous year. Within this we constructed a robust visitor walkway, that would be able safely to accommodate at least one coach load, of about 55 people. One wall of this building is 1m (3ft) taller than the other. This taller wall stands in the old excavation trench; this arrangement ensures that damage, caused by the steel stakes that pin the building to the ground, is kept to a minimum. The smart new shelter allowed us to excavate a far larger area, and under almost ideal conditions.

We finished work within the Swedish shelter in 1996. That winter a terrible storm ripped the cover which was now almost ten years old. So the following summer we removed the few remaining posts and abandoned the excavation. This coincided with construction of the new Preservation Hall, where visitors could now see waterlogged timbers *in situ*, all year round. For the past ten years our excavations have been smaller in scale and we have never had the resources necessary to mount a large-scale excavation of the deeper and better preserved timbers. But that does not mean that they are not under threat. Soon, but only if we can raise the funds, we will have to grasp that nettle.

OUR IDEAS BEGIN TO CHANGE

The three types of layer first identified in 1984 were again encountered in the new trench. The highest layer consisted of an apparent 'collapse'; below this was a sandy floor, with foundations of stouter timbers below that. The timbers of what we still believed was a building continued in four rows, as we had seen on the dykeside trench, with 'eaves-support posts' on the south side (the north side was outside the excavation). Again, we encountered mortised planks and other pieces that had been pegged down – one timber had been secured in place by no less than 14 small pegs. There could be no doubt that the floor and lower timbers had been carefully placed in position.

The higher levels produced surprises, too. Just outside another entranceway in the south wall were several large oak timbers, including a plank with mortice holes at each end and a large, unused post with a characteristic pencil-like tip, which this time was not coated with clay (colour plate 13). Its other end, the top, which was intact, had been carefully fashioned into a flat shoulder with a prominent, long tenon (45). This post (which we labelled B61) was probably about to be used to replace an eaves-support, when water levels rose and the small dump of what looked like timber 'builder's supplies' was abandoned outside the supposed building.

There was one additional surprise in store for us after we had opened to the public. It was made to one side of our visitors' car park, in rough grass, where we accidentally came across numerous oak timbers, deeply buried beneath the surface. The tool marks were identical to the ones we had been looking at for years at Flag Fen, and there was no reason to doubt that this new discovery was part of the Bronze Age timber platform. We realised that if these timbers were indeed part of the same platform, then it must be almost a third as large again as we had originally estimated. It was a daunting prospect.

Finds from excavations since 1987 have included large amounts of pottery, including a complete pot of Middle Bronze Age type, another, bigger shale bracelet fragment, a somewhat decayed small bronze knife or dagger with three rivets, a ball-headed bronze stick pin and many animal bones (colour plate 14). At first glance, this collection of material looks ordinary enough, but is it? The pottery, for instance, generally joins together if one makes the effort to restore it, and this is not what one would expect of a 'normal' domestic site. Two of the vessels were found almost complete and one had undoubtedly been deliberately placed in the ground underneath the floor, because a log had been pegged into position above it and yet the fragile pot beneath was undamaged. Whole pots are sometimes found on domestic sites, but complete daggers are certainly very unusual.

Most of the finds from Flag Fen were straightforwardly Late Bronze Age in appearance, but the complete jar found beneath the log, which had been embellished with pinched-up decoration around the belly, and the dagger with three rivets could equally well date to the Middle Bronze Age. To be more precise: the Late Bronze Age finds post-date 1000 BC, while the Middle Bronze ones pre-date it by a century or two. So far only two metalwork finds from the timber platform at Flag Fen are demonstrably post-Bronze Age. The first is a safety pin-style brooch of the later Iron Age which was found on the south side of the posts, but at a significantly higher level than the Bronze Age items. We once regarded this Iron Age brooch as an accidental loss: perhaps something mislaid in the water after a pleasant afternoon's picnic in the Fens. Just how wrong we were, was shown by the discovery, in July 1992, of a damaged bronze

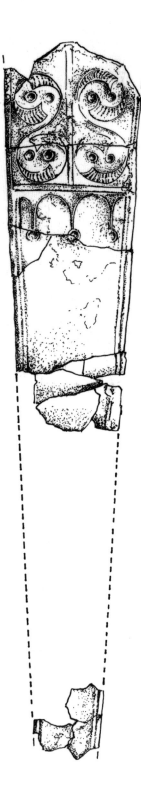

45 Drawing by Jenny Coombs of the decorated
scabbard plate for an Iron Age short sword found
in July 1992, in peat just above the highest level
of timbers at Flag Fen. Like other Bronze Age
scabbards six to seven centuries before it, this
third-century BC scabbard had been deliberately
damaged. *From* The Flag Fen Basin Report, *courtesy
of English Heritage*

46 A complete oak post found in the 'dump' of unused timbers on the south side of the post alignment (*see colour plate 13*). Note the long pencil-like tip and the long tenon at the other end. It is possible that this post could have come from a construction project on dry land

plate that once formed the outside of an Iron Age short sword's scabbard (*46*). This plate had been finely decorated with Celtic Art and was an object of great beauty. Despite this, it had been deliberately bent and broken.

The discovery of the Iron Age sword scabbard plate is important for several reasons. First, it is a beautiful object in itself. Second, the style of art and the shape of the plate can be dated quite precisely to the third century BC. Finally, the way it was treated, by being bent and broken is exactly what had been happening to sword scabbards at Flag Fen for six or seven centuries.

EVERYTHING CHANGES: THE POWER STATION EXCAVATIONS, 1989

The story began conventionally enough in the early summer of 1987. We had employed a contractor to dig a trench for the water main which was to service our first visitor centre, which was a temporary tent-like structure. This pipe was routed from the end of Fourth Drove, along the canalised Cat's Water, along the Roman road and thence to the visitor centre. We treated this as an opportunity to put an archaeological trench straight across most of Flag Fen, and so we kept a very close eye on operations.

As the work progressed, we noted that there were oak posts in the trench where it skirted our car park; these were heading, it seemed, in the direction of Fengate. I immediately wondered whether this could be the causeway we had hoped to find, which would have linked the Flag Fen timber platform to the dry land at Fengate? It looked very promising so I kept my fingers crossed. A few days later, as the digger started to work parallel to the Cat's Water dyke, we knew that something might well happen – and it did. One day we spotted the decayed remains of posts in the pipe-trench, about 200m west of the Roman road, close to a belt of trees that marks the edge of Peterborough New Town.

As soon as the machine revealed the first posts, we immediately fitted it with a wide, toothless bucket, and gently cleared an area about 3m (10ft) wide and 20m (66ft) long, between the water main and the Cat's Water ditch. This trench revealed nearly 30 posts, mostly of split oak, together with a number of oak planks which seemed to be *in situ*. It was all very reminiscent of the Flag Fen platform to the east, but on a much smaller scale. Sadly, too, it was very much drier. Preservation was nowhere near as good. Although it is always difficult to make sense of a small trench, the posts did seem to be heading towards our car park and the main Flag Fen platform excavation beyond it. In short, it really did seem that we had found the long-lost causeway.

We took six samples for radiocarbon dating from the new trench and sent them to Cambridge University; three of the samples were from posts, three from planks near the posts. The results showed beyond reasonable doubt that the sampled posts and planks were of the same date, in the Late Bronze Age.

Two years later I was approached by the City Council Planning Department about a proposed power station that was to be built immediately north and west of the Cat's Water. The land in question was one of the lowest-lying fields in Fengate and it was plain that the posts we had found in 1987, if they were indeed part of a causeway, *must* run across a large part of it. We put this idea to the developers, Hawker Siddeley Power Engineering Ltd, who agreed to fund an exploratory excavation.

We started the dig in April 1989 and finished it in October, after one of the hottest, driest summers on record – not ideal conditions for a wetland dig. However, the results were spectacular. We encountered the posts where we had expected, and excavated a long, trench across the site of the future power station to expose them (47). They ran in a band about 10-12m (33-40ft) wide and some 150m (495ft) long, from the lowest-lying area, where they were still relatively well preserved, to the higher gravel of the Fen-margin proper, where all that was left were just a few brown stains and smears of peat-like powder that had once been wood.

We decided to extend the original trench westwards, towards the dry land, but first we had to determine the precise level to which we would strip mechanically. This was a very difficult decision. The overburden consisted of more than 1m (3ft) of very stiff, river-borne clay alluvium, and spade- or mattock-digging through this was out of the question. On the other hand, if we went too deep with the

47 A view of the power station excavations, from the top of a fire engine's ladder. This initial trench was later enlarged. One of the first hand-cut trenches through the post alignment is visible under black plastic in the foreground. The paler gravel of the Fengate fen-edge is visible at the far end of the trench

machine we would damage the posts, particularly their upper portions which, as we will see, were especially important. So we stayed as high as we could, but were aware of the fact that we would only expose a limited proportion of the actual posts in the alignment.

As soon as I saw the first few posts exposed in a hand-dug trench I was convinced that our 'causeway' was not just a simple route across wet ground (*48*). It seemed far too elaborate for that, and besides, we knew what prehistoric trackways looked like because many were then being superbly excavated in the Somerset Levels. If it wasn't just a simple trackway I still had no idea what it actually could have been. So I opted for a non-specific term to describe it, and the name 'post alignment' seems to have stuck.

We employed several machines to clear the enlarged area and they finished work in early summer, by which time we had exposed nearly 800 posts of which over 95 per cent were of oak. We then placed hand-cut trenches across the alignment and to nobody's surprise more than doubled the number of posts that comprised the post alignment. We would now estimate that the total number of posts on the power station sub-site alone is well over 2000. The new posts that appeared in the hand-cut sections were generally smaller than the others, and

48 Two hand-cut trenches in the power station excavations. Most of the posts surviving at this level are in oak (2m scales)

this probably explains why they had not survived higher up in the soil. The post alignment on the power station field was wider, by about 2-3m (6-9ft) than at Flag Fen, and the posts were generally smaller.

At this point in the excavation it became apparent that the post alignment headed straight towards Flag Fen (*49*). We also knew that there were posts west of our artificial lake, beside the car park under the visitor centre and at two points on the lake's circumference. The posts then ran across the platform, through the main excavations, and presumably across the field on the east side of the Mustdyke, perhaps for 200m up to the gravel shores of Northey 'island'. In all, there was probably 900m, perhaps even a full kilometre of posts. It was an extraordinary thought.

The upright timbers in the main Flag Fen excavation were on the same orientation as the posts of the alignment, and it was now obvious that the house or building hypothesis was completely untenable. The Flag Fen structure was part of the post alignment – end of story. But that still did not explain the objects that we found there. Was this just debris that had accumulated along a track? Given the nature of what we had found – weaponry, complete pots, etc – that hardly seemed probable. We knew that there must be some other explanation.

49 Aerial view of Flag Fen in 1995, from a hot air balloon. In the distance are the buildings of modern Fengate with the power station closest to the fen-edge. Its two huge fuel tanks are clearly visible. The road across Flag Fen more or less follows the post alignment. The Mere, the old Visitor Centre and the curve of the Mustdyke can be seen in the foreground

THE SIGNIFICANCE OF TREE-RINGS

The dating and chronology of Flag Fen has depended a great deal on the technique of tree-ring analysis. The principles behind dendrochronology, as it is known in archaeology, are now generally well known. Basically the technique depends on the simple fact that trees lay down wider growth-rings in good growing (usually wet) years than in poor ones. The width of each annual growth ring is measured through a microscope, to an accuracy of about a hundredth of a millimetre. The resulting graph of ring dimensions is then fed into a computer, which already has information on tree-ring widths over the past 8,000 years. The machine compares the new data with the existing graph and – hey presto – out pops a date. That, at least, is the principle; but there are snags.

Some trees, such as alder for example, may lay down two rings in a year, others grow slowly for most of the year and do not reflect the seasons. So the technique is mainly applied to oak and pine, although ash can also be dated, and alder is reputed to be nearly sorted out in certain laboratories.

The 'dendro' dating at Flag Fen was done on site by Janet Neve who joined us in 1984 after graduating in archaeology from Manchester University. Being a young and very poor project, we were not able to offer Janet an instant and fully fitted laboratory; but instead we rented a portable office and bought ourselves a small computer. Janet then had the job of putting together the dendrometer, the machine that did the actual measuring, which was built for us by students at Peterborough Regional College from pieces of an RAF jet fighter, (among other things). The all-important software was kindly given to us by Dr Pilcher then at the Queen's University, Belfast.

Knowing what we know now we probably wouldn't have attempted to assemble a tree-ring laboratory on a shoestring, but we did; eventually, and with invaluable help from Cathy Groves of the Sheffield University dendro lab we actually came up with a series of dates. But to get that far we had to assemble a brand-new 'curve' or series of dates for eastern England, because it was impossible to match the growth patterns of trees from Flag Fen and those grown further west, in Somerset for example. In actual fact the new Flag Fen curve worked out by Janet and her friends in Sheffield is very important because it links the British curve with that of the Low Countries and Germany. It has also been an essential building block for recent developments in the tree-ring sequences of eastern England. The dates show (and I quote from Janet and Cathy's chapter (8) in the Flag Fen Basin Report):

> that there was probably a period of major construction activity in the first half of the thirteenth century BC, followed by a lull … Construction activity appears to have increased again at the turn of the twelfth century BC, to have carried on throughout the eleventh century BC, and into the early part of the tenth century BC. Activity then tails off during the tenth century and appears to have stopped around the turn of the tenth century.

The dendrochronology suggests that tree felling for Flag Fen began just after 1300 BC, at the very end of the Middle Bronze Age. There was then a pause, presumably because water levels remained stable. Then, around 1200 BC, rebuilding began in earnest, to end around 900 BC, when condition were becoming very wet. At this point, although rebuilding in timber seems to have ceased, we know from the wealth of Iron Age finds (mostly from the power station excavations) that the post alignment was visited and revisited, right up until early Roman times.

The summer of 1989 blazed on, and we had terrible problems trying to keep hundreds of posts wet across the huge power station open-area excavation. A routine, however, soon became established once we had secured the expert services of a small team of experienced excavators sub-contracted from the Lincoln Trust. The small team at the power station dug and recorded the wood using the Flag Fen system. Several times every day poor Maisie and Janet ran from Flag Fen to the power station and back again, in ever-decreasing circles, sampling, soaking and wrapping wood; but they survived – and were the fitter for it.

THE DISCOVERY OF METALWORK AT THE POWER STATION

Contrary to some archaeological opinion, I have always maintained that the vast majority of metal-detector users are honest people caught up in an absorbing hobby. Those who break the law are rogues and should be treated as such, but most are honestly doing amateur archaeology of a specialised sort. Rather than fight each other, archaeologists and metal-detector users should try to work together.

Relations between the local Soke Metal Detector Club and Fenland Archaeological Trust (the charitable trust that runs Flag Fen) had long been friendly. So in the spring of 1989 I invited the club to the power station site, as part of a normal routine visit. But this time I had a hunch that something remarkable was going to happen. Bronze Age metalwork and wet sites have long been known to go together, and before the search started, I told the group that they were looking for swords and daggers. I said it tongue-in-cheek and it got a good laugh, but ten minutes later the laughter died when the first find, a complete Bronze Age sword, was revealed in the silts, just to one side of the posts (50).

50 The first metal-detector find at the power station was this Late Bronze Age Wilburton sword (with hilt to the right). The remains of the blade, which has broken across a casting flaw, was found nearby. Scale in cm

51 The skeleton of a Labrador-sized dog found at the power station site. It would seem that its lower back and hips had been pierced by an oak post of the alignment

This spectacular find did wonders for my credibility. I cannot attempt to recount the discovery of the power station metalwork piece by piece, as it all runs together in my mind as a bewildering, sun-baked, dusty rush around the site, desperately trying to keep on top of the mapping and note-taking. The club came back on the following five weekends and on every visit they found fresh material. By the first week in June we had recovered nearly 60 objects, including two complete and two fragmentary swords, numerous pins and other items, including an extraordinary pair of Iron Age shears and their fitted wooden box.

While the detecting was going on, the regular archaeological crew had also found two dog burials, one of which had been pierced by a post (*51*), and a human skeleton which lay some distance north of the post alignment. I would guess that this skeleton, which was actually little more than a chalky stain in the silts was probably Iron Age and a few centuries later than the posts of the alignment. Most of the metal finds from around or near the posts were Late Bronze Age, but a significant number dated to the Early Iron Age – perhaps around 400-500 BC.

The metalwork finds were of great interest to David Keys of *The Independent* newspaper and he wrote a big report which appeared on 24 June 1989. The story attracted widespread attention and did wonders to the Flag Fen visitor numbers, but it also caused, as I had anticipated, security problems on the power station excavation. I knew we were being visited by 'nighthawks', but I don't think they got away with much – if anything. We never finished a day's work without an exhaustive metal-detector search and were at pains to remove everything of any value from the ground before we went home.

The first enlarged trench had still concentrated on the area around the post alignment, but throughout the summer finds of metalwork were occurring at the very edge of the excavation. So by late summer I decided it was time to expand the trench and, if needs be, on a huge scale. This was going to be very expensive, so we called on English Heritage who were able to provide the large cheques we needed to pay the earth-moving bills. Our research design was elegant in its simplicity: keep removing earth until the spread of archaeological finds stopped. That would be the only way we could determine how sites like Flag Fen operated in the Bronze Age.

So instead of loosely linking finds with posts, we could now be quite specific about their pattern of deposition, which tended to favour the boundary between the wet and dry ground. They were also arranged in a band which extended for about 30m to the south (but not to the north) of the post alignment (52-54). This

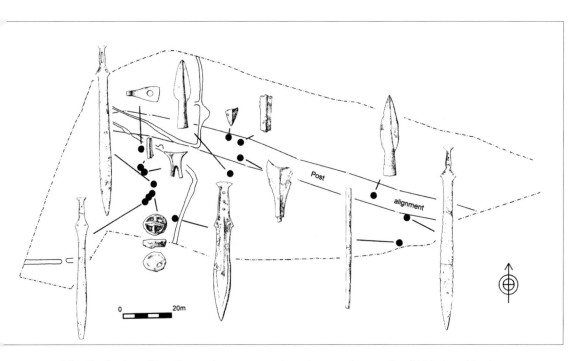

52 The distribution of Late Bronze Age weaponry (swords, a sword pommel, a shield tab, scabbard chapes, spearheads and spear ferrules) at the power station excavations. The edges of the post alignment are indicated by a dot-and-dash line. *From* The Flag Fen Basin Report, *courtesy of English Heritage*

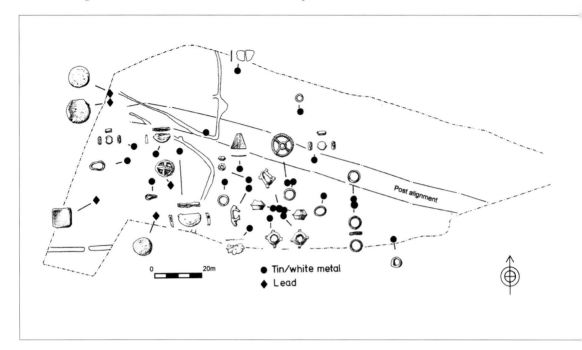

53 The distribution of Late Bronze Age objects in lead and white metal at the power station excavations. The edges of the post alignment are indicated by a dot-and-dash line. *From* The Flag Fen Basin Report, *courtesy of English Heritage*

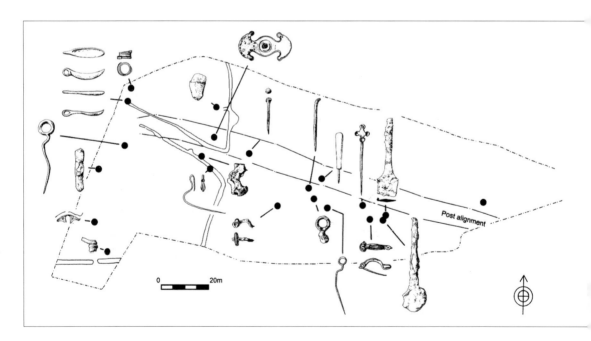

54 The distribution of Iron Age objects at the power station excavations. The edges of the post alignment are indicated by a dot-and-dash line. *From* The Flag Fen Basin Report, *courtesy of English Heritage*

would suggest that people came up to the posts from the 'inland' or 'protected' side of the posts to make their deposits. It also hints at the fact that the open or northerly side of the posts was considered somehow unfriendly, or hostile – an idea that finds support from the occurrence of the Iron Age body there.

Even today, no soil-searching techniques can detect artefacts below more than 1m (3ft) of overburden, so we had no practical alternatives but to dig. The power station could not be delayed, so we had to move fast. By the end of October we had cleared an area of about 2ha (5 acres), with the posts running more or less down the centre. As I have noted, when we plotted the metalwork, it was concentrated along one side of the posts only. This completely ruled out the notion that the finds represented 'casual loss' from a road or raised causeway. Even if we allow the (absurd) idea that Bronze Age people were the ultimate litter louts, one would expect 'casual losses' off a road to be evenly spread on either side.

Some of the items had been placed in the water about 30m (99ft) from the posts, and it has been suggested that they might have been thrown there from a platform above the posts. I do not think this likely, however, because while many of the items had been broken, often broken pieces from the same object were found in the ground together – sometimes even touching. This could only happen if they had either been placed, or carefully dropped, in the water, probably from a boat.

The majority of items showed clear evidence of damage, indeed the conservator at the British Museum, Simon Dove, described it to me as prehistoric 'vandalism': pins were snapped in half; decorative inlay was smashed off; blades were bent and so on. One example will suffice. The late Dr David Coombs of Manchester University was an old friend and an acknowledged expert on Late Bronze Age metalwork. So when we started to excavate his subject matter by the sackful I turned to him for help.

Every few weekends he would call in to see what we had found. One Sunday morning he paid a flying visit and found us on site excavating around a metal-detector's very strong non-ferrous signal. Dave's doctoral thesis was on British Late Bronze Age metalwork, and he has seen many thousands of bronzes, but this was the first time he had actually seen an axe come out of the ground; this is because Bronze Age metalwork is very rarely found in archaeological excavations: the vast majority are found by farmers, detectorists, quarrymen or contractors' workmen going about their daily business.

The bronze socketed axe that Dave and I excavated was in perfect condition and showed no signs of the 'vandalism' noted elsewhere – at least that is what we thought at first. But when we started to examine the wood round about the axe head we soon saw that the two-piece handle had been smashed, leaving the axe itself intact. If one pauses to think about it, an axe is a difficult thing to smash – almost as hard as a hammer – so they smashed the handle. Then they buried both together in a small muddy scoop below the water. These were small-scale, perhaps private, rites. They do not seem to have been large-scale public ceremonies.

So, to sum up, the metalwork from the power station was found using detectors, a technique which is largely unbiased. The distribution of metalwork as revealed by the detectors is therefore a true reflection of its original spread in antiquity. The vast majority of metal finds were among, and to one side of, the posts. Again, most of the items were deliberately damaged and many had been carefully dropped, rather than thrown into the water. These observations point indisputably to the fact that the metalwork, if nothing else, was deliberately removed from daily life by being ritually destroyed. Its deposition within the waters of Flag Fen was a symbolic way of marking its passage to another realm – perhaps that of the ancestors or the afterlife.

THE POWER STATION FINDS

The majority of metal items were in bronze, an alloy, usually composed of about 10 per cent tin and 90 per cent copper (brass, introduced to Britain in Roman times, also contains zinc). In all, the power station excavation revealed just under 300 metal objects, of which the large majority were pins, rings and ornaments. The greatest weight of metal, however, was in weapons: swords, dirks, daggers and a rapier (*colour plate 15*). Tools were relatively rare, apart from a collection of almost 20 tanged chisels, punches and awls which were found in the same area and probably represent an individual craftsman's tool kit.

Most of the metalwork can be dated to the Late Bronze Age and belong to a well-defined style, group or 'industry' named after the Fenland village of Wilburton, a few miles north of Cambridge. Wilburton itself is on an old 'island', but the wet fen around it has produced large quantities of Late Bronze Age metalwork, in a very distinctive style – and nearly all of it, I am quite convinced, was put there on purpose. Two complete Wilburton swords were found at the power station, together with fragments of others, and broken pieces of scabbard fittings. There was also a complete, but broken, Early Iron Age sword (technically of La Tène I type, fourth and fifth centuries BC) and pieces from others.

The collection of smaller blade weapons was extraordinary, ranging from a complete Middle Bronze Age rapier, via sundry Late Bronze Age dirks and daggers to what can only be described as a miniature Wilburton sword. Late Bronze Age spears were less plentifully represented, but one spearhead, although partially sharpened, was nonetheless incomplete, as the socket for its shaft was still filled with mould material; others still had pieces of wooden shaft in their sockets. The non-business end of many Bronze Age spear shafts were sometimes shod with a ferrule, rather like a walking stick. These are generally quite small, but one very unusual large, broken example was also found at the power station.

It has been suggested that many Late Bronze Age shields and weapons found in bogs, fens and rivers were not functional. Professor John Coles has convincingly shown that the shafts of large spearheads were often too small to be used, and the thin bronze of shields would simply buckle and rip if struck hard by a Bronze Age sword. The same must apply to sheet bronze helmets, too. Possible fragments from one, and maybe two helmets were found and these would be the first examples from Britain. Again, they were smashed, and this makes it difficult to be certain about their identification. David Coombs was more convinced when he first saw them, but seemed to change his mind in the metalwork chapter of the Flag Fen Basin Report.

The most unusual find was a pair of sprung bronze shears in a carefully carved, fitted wooden box which had a little slot in the base for a sharpening stone (*colour plate 16*). These shears are probably of Iron Age date and can be used for shearing or cutting many things, from human hair or wool to thin willow osiers. They were unique in bronze, until the recent (2004) discovery of a decorated example from Hamperden End, in Essex. The decoration places the Essex shears to the later Iron Age, around 20 BC–AD 70. It's hard to be certain, but I would place the Flag Fen shears somewhat earlier in the Iron Age.

The power station excavations also revealed an array of broken Bronze Age pins, mostly of stick type and with disc heads, some of which were decorated. Various rings in bronze and tin could have been ornaments or harness fittings and are entirely characteristic of the Late Bronze Age Wilburton tradition. Early Iron Age brooches, pins and ornaments were also bent, twisted or otherwise deliberately damaged, but were very high class objects, often with provision for inlaid decoration of tin, glass or coral – all of which, sadly, had been smashed out (*colour plate 17*). It is perhaps worth noting that some of the Iron Age fine brooches are the type of item one would normally expect to find in a well-furnished, elite warrior grave.

Arguably the most remarkable ornament was again smashed. Being unique it is hard to date at this stage, other than to state that it is probably Bronze Age. It is a large bracelet or armlet (a bracelet worn on the upper arm) of shale, but deeply inlaid with lead, which has been applied in strips (*colour plate 18*). The decoration of bands, lozenges and chevrons is distinctly Bronze Age and can best be paralleled by a remarkable inlaid shale bowl of probable Late Bronze Age date, from Caergwrle, now in the National Museum of Wales. It is an exceptionally fine object.

Another extraordinary aspect of the power station discoveries was the fact that a surprisingly high proportion of the metal finds are made from pure metallic tin (*colour plate 17*). This has not been noted before in Britain, but is probably due to the site's naturally waterlogged conditions (which impede corrosion) and the fact that most tin items are very small and are unlikely to be spotted with the naked eye. Other tiny finds included individual bronze rivets from swords and daggers. These again indicate a degree of deliberate smashing and their discovery amply justifies the use of metal-detectors.

A crucible fragment that had been used to melt pure tin, was found on the Iron Age Cat's Water settlement, just south of the power station, in 1975. This could indicate that some of the power station finds were made locally, perhaps for the sole purpose of 'sacrifice' to the waters. This suggestion might seem ridiculous were it not for the fact that many of the metal objects, such as the bronze swords, were clearly rather second-rate castings. We have already referred to the spearhead with mould material still in its socket, but at least two of the swords had been broken across major casting flaws and one must ask whether they could ever have been used in actual battle. Similarly the miniature Wilburton sword is too tiny to be an efficient fighting weapon. Could it be that much of this material was actually manufactured on site with deposition and ceremonial breakage in mind?

It would be a mistake to give the impression that metalwork was the only material found at the power station sub-site. There were many animal bones, often of dogs, and numerous pot sherds, too. Whether these were deposited in the water along with the metalwork remains to be seen, however.

Death was a recurrent theme. We have already mentioned a body, found on the north-eastern side of the posts, and two thigh bones of a fairly tall person were also found on that side, but some way away from the articulated bones. At one point an area of posts had been used to dispose of loose human bones; over three individuals are represented and with the bones we found a broken shale bracelet and a complete boar's tusk; these must surely be offerings of some sort and were probably associated with rites of passage to do with death.

THE POST ALIGNMENT RECONSIDERED

We now know for a fact that the post alignment ran for over a kilometre from Fengate to Northey. We have had to discard our original ideas about long houses and domestic life. Even the attractive 'lake village' idea has had to go. But how are we to explain the various clues that led us astray in the first place? Let us take each one separately, starting with the one which first struck us so forcibly back in 1983 and '84: the coarse white sand. The answer here is that it was indeed dusted on a floor to make it less slippery, but that floor does not have to have been within a building. It could just as well have been on a causeway or path.

The cavity 'walls' would have been more convincing if we had found clear evidence for daub coatings of some sort (although this was not noted on the Dutch examples which we know for a fact belonged to houses). My current feeling is that these wattle structures were actually revetments which were placed along the outside of the post alignment, maybe to hold a filling of peat and brushwood, most of which has subsequently been lost.

As we worked inside the large Swedish shelter, where conditions actually allowed us to think about what we were excavating, it became increasingly clear that the post alignment was both a causeway and a barrier. It was also a ritual site, possibly only at certain times of the year, but more on that shortly. Apart from the dump of unused timbers, the upper levels showed evidence for disturbance, perhaps by water. Maybe some form of superstructure – such as hand rails – had collapsed (*colour plate 19*). At one point the causeway passed close by a small area of open water with a massive tangentially-split oak plank to one side; maybe this served as hard-standing or a landing stage of some sort (*colour plate 20*). Below the rather tumbled timbers of Level 1 we encountered evidence in Levels 2-4 for a series of paths or walkways on either side of the central Row 3, of posts (*colour plate 21*). These surfaces were made from sand, small planks and woodchips, often mixed with potsherds. In the lowest levels the walkways became harder to define, but planks appeared to have been used to cross particularly wet and boggy patches of ground (*colour plate 22*).

The presence of conjoining potsherds or complete pottery vessels from the post alignment can be explained in terms of deliberate 'offerings'; the same can be said for conjoining shale bracelet fragments. Offerings were by no means confined to the higher levels. Four examples of complete and lightly used quernstones were found beneath the lowest timbers of the post alignment within the Flag Fen platform (*colour plate 23*) and these probably provide the clue that explains the meaning of the pottery and other seemingly domestic material. I would suggest that these, rather like a complete quernstone we found at the much earlier Neolithic (3800 BC) causewayed enclosure at Etton, were *symbols* of domesticity and family life, rather than evidence for actual domestic activity (*colour plates 24* and *25*).

The tree-ring sequence gave us broad dates for phases of activity, but we encountered problems when it came to the linking of these general episodes of building and rebuilding to the actual timbers themselves. This failure to provide a tightly dated structural sequence reflected the fact that most of the dated timbers were posts that had been driven down from the top. Further problems were caused by the fact that many of the posts had lost their bark and much of their sapwood, which made it impossible to arrive at actual dates, rather than date ranges. Even so we able to make a reasonably well-informed guess at the development of the post alignment between 1300 and 900 BC. In short, after a slow start (55: phase 1) the structure grows in complexity and a remarkable robust corduroy-like layer of timbers, known as the 'log layer' was laid down early in Phase 3 (56) to act as a foundation that was not likely to sink (57). The layers above the 'log layer' were a succession of walkways, mostly on either side of Row 3. The scattering of posts known as Row 4 may actually have formed an irregular wall or palisade of posts (in the middle of the third phase). The post alignment reverted to a simple footpath in its latest phase (58). There were also indications for an unexpected partitioning or transverse element in at least one place where the post alignment crossed the platform. This may have been a structural necessity, but other explanations (which I will discuss in the next section) are also possible.

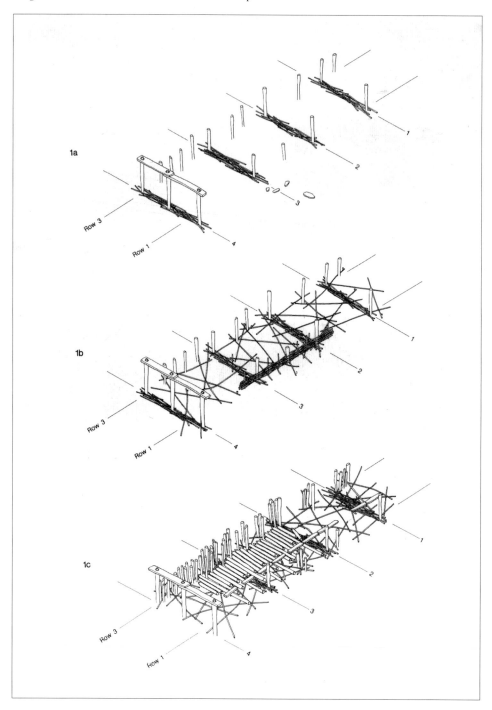

55 Schematic reconstruction by Colin Irons showing the first phase of development of the Flag Fen post alignment as a causeway. *From* The Flag Fen Basin Report, *courtesy of English Heritage*

56 Photo-montage of the Flag Fen 'log layer' in Level 5. *From* The Flag Fen Basin Report, *courtesy of English Heritage*

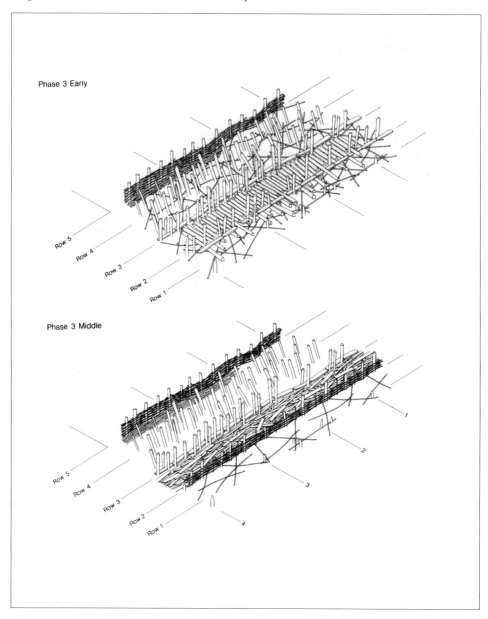

Phase 3 Early

Row 5
Row 4
Row 3
Row 2
Row 1

Phase 3 Middle

Row 5
Row 4
Row 3
Row 2
Row 1

57 Schematic reconstruction by Colin Irons showing the middle phases of development of the Flag Fen post alignment as a causeway. *From* The Flag Fen Basin Report, *courtesy of English Heritage*

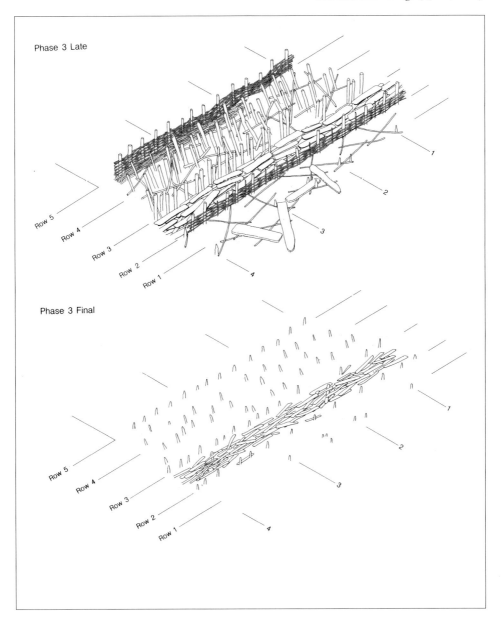

Phase 3 Late

Row 5
Row 4
Row 3
Row 2
Row 1

Phase 3 Final

Row 5
Row 4
Row 3
Row 2
Row 1

58 Schematic reconstruction by Colin Irons showing the later phases of development of the Flag Fen post alignment as a causeway. *From* The Flag Fen Basin Report, *courtesy of English Heritage*

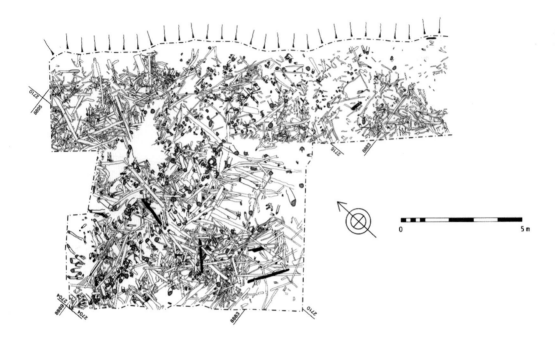

59 Flag Fen excavations: the distribution of oak timbers (in black) at the highest level (1). *From* The Flag Fen Basin Report, *courtesy of English Heritage*

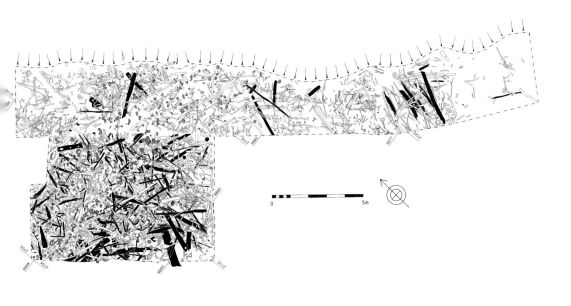

60 Flag Fen excavations: the distribution of oak timbers (in black) at the lowest level (*5*). *From* The Flag Fen Basin Report, *courtesy of English Heritage*

It was not until we had completed most of the post-excavation analyses, by 1996, that we were able to plot the types of wood used at Flag Fen. The main conclusion was that fenland species, such as alder and willow, occurred most frequently in the earliest phases of the structure (*59*). It was not until later that oak began to be used at all frequently (*60*). This is not what one would have expected and may reflect the site's growing importance, because oak is a valuable structural timber, which could not have been grown in the wetland itself, and must have been transported to Flag Fen, either from the higher ground in the immediate vicinity, or from further afield. The preponderance of fenland species lower down in the sequence doubtless reflects the fact that the alder carr woods around the edges of the Flag Fen basin had to be cleared, before construction of the post alignment and platform could begin.

At this point it might be as well to pause and think further about Bronze Age woodworking. We saw earlier how efficient saws with opposed teeth had yet to be invented and how most division of timber was by splitting 'green' wood. Bronze axes are a great improvement on stone ones, but they still are best used on 'green' oak. I have tried working seasoned oak with a bronze axe, but it was a hopeless task. One look at some of the woodworking at Flag Fen showed how

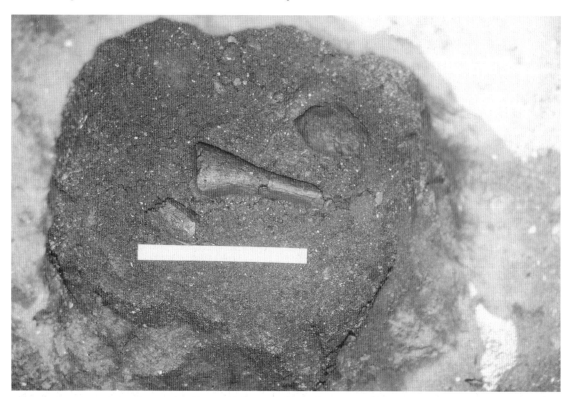

63 A complete 'hook' style haft for a socketed axe in the lowest level of wood at Flag Fen

61 *Opposite above:* The smashed remains of a Late Bronze Age two-piece axe haft from the power station excavations. The socketed axe that went with the broken haft was found a few centimetres below it. Scale 30cm (1ft)

62 *Opposite below:* Reconstruction of the axe haft shown in 61. The main shaft is made from a half-split ash log and the smaller fore-shaft on which the axe is fitted is in willow. The axe is secured to the haft by twine which passes through the loop on the axe

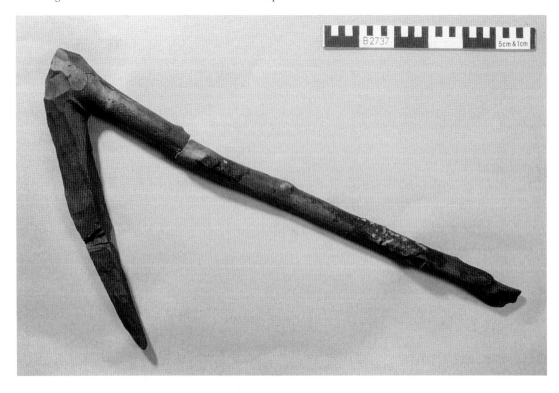

64 The axe haft seen in 63. The nick roughly halfway along the pointed hook, was for tying twine to retain the axehead, should it fly off during use

it had to have been done when the wood was freshly felled and 'green' (*colour plate 26*). But it was not as simple as that, because we now know that although axeheads could be very similar, the manner of their hafting could make a big difference to the way they were used.

I was able to make a reconstruction of the broken axe haft found at the power station (*61*). This two-piece haft had the main shaft made from a half-split ash log (*62*). Into this was inserted a smaller willow 'fore-shaft', which fitted into the socketed axe (the only type of axe used at Flag Fen). An altogether different type of haft was the 'hook' type. We found one of these, without its head, in the lowest level of timber at Flag Fen (*63*). It was split out of an oak tree trunk and a side branch formed the handle (*64*). The socketed axe fitted over the pointed tip of the hook. There were two deep nicks on either side, just above the top of the spot where the axe fitted on (which we could tell by the way the wood had been bruised). These nicks were to secure a string, which passed through a loop on the side of the axehead.

Phil Harding and I did some experiments for Maisie as part of a *Time Team Special* on a Bronze Age site at Washingborough in the Witham valley, just outside Lincoln. We reckoned that the two-piece haft made for a good felling axe – or even a battle axe. The 'hook' haft was better at working hazel coppice and a shorter version of the 'hook' haft (which we have also found at Flag Fen) made an excellent tool for axing-through mortice holes in planks. We concluded that it was the shape of the haft, rather than the axehead itself, which determined how it was used.

There was abundant evidence for carpentry at Flag Fen and Maisie Taylor has written a large chapter about it in the Flag Fen Basin Report. Coppice was worked there, but most of the woodworking was of heavier timber and it was also hard to avoid the conclusion that much of the worked timber (65) had been taken from houses or other structures – presumably once they had fallen into disrepair. Maisie was also surprised to find much evidence for beaver. It was clear that beavers were both eating wood and using it to make the lodges where they lived (66). Bronze Age Flag Fen would have been a very different place from what it has become today.

So, what *was* the post alignment? First and foremost it was undoubtedly a causeway or trackway across the wetland that separated Fengate from Northey 'island'. But it was also a barrier that separated the Flag Fen basin from the open

65 A selection of timbers with slots and mortices. It is probable that many of these had been reused or salvaged from structures on dry land

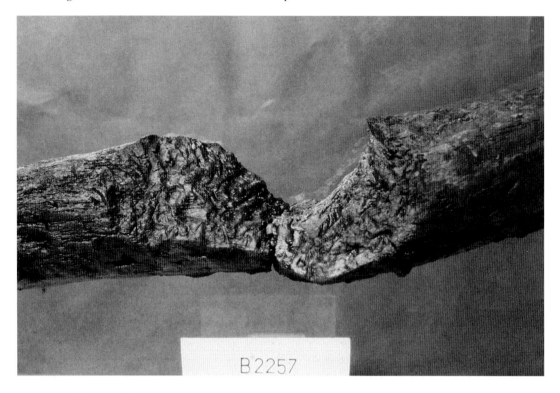

66 Alder wood from Flag Fen showing clear evidence for gnawing by beaver

fen to the north and east. Flag Fen was a naturally enclosed basin, which was surrounded by the fields and settlements of Northey, Fengate and Bradley Fen – a recently discovered new Bronze Age settlement complex on the northern side of Whittlesey 'island'.★ All were within clear sight of the Flag Fen post alignment and platform. The wetland basin would have 'belonged to' and have been controlled by these people. It was a vitally important resource that had to be protected: a source of winter protein, summer grazing, peat, reeds, firewood and salt. Plainly they did not want people from outside to have access to it. This might help to explain the mass of posts used in the northern part of the post alignment (especially Row 4). But the posts also seem to have had another, less practical, role – which is what I will consider next.

★See *Britain BC*, pp.289-93

RELIGION AND CEREMONIAL

Common sense, if nothing else, suggests that the deposition of so much metalwork, not to mention complete pots, smashed shale bracelets and unused quernstones, must have been deliberate. And the only explanation for such seemingly impractical, senseless destruction or waste of valuable resources has to be something to do with religion, ceremonial or ritual. Moreover, these 'offerings' were also taking place on a large scale: Flag Fen must have been more than a purely local shrine. So if it be accepted that Flag Fen and the power station were parts of a religious centre of some sort, we must next consider what might have been happening there. In other words, what did these religious rites comprise?

The metalwork at the power station is principally composed of weapons and ornaments. Further east, out in the basin proper at Flag Fen we have so far found one Iron Age brooch, a late Iron Age sword scabbard plate, a Late Bronze Age sword scabbard chape (or tip), a Late Bronze Age stick pin, a Late or Middle Bronze Age dagger, a so-called 'flesh-hook' and two leaf-shaped bronze spearheads. We have also found evidence either for the reuse of parts of vehicles, or for their dismantling and deliberate incorporation into the post alignment as offerings. So far we have found part of a tripartite wooden wheel (*colour plate 27*), in the lower levels, and therefore dating to shortly after 1300 BC and two axles, all from different vehicles (*67*). Our most recent excavations on the extreme edge of the Northey shore have revealed rings, like those found at the power station, and a bronze harness-fitting, or slide for a strap, which can be closely paralleled in a hoard of Late Bronze Age metal objects found at Parc-y-Meirch, Denbighshire.

As at the power station, these finds were amongst the posts or on their south-western side. The other distinctive items common to the two areas are smashed shale bracelets. At Flag Fen, too, we have evidence for careful deposition of pottery.

It has been suggested that there are fewer metalwork finds at Flag Fen than at the power station, but in fact the former has produced slightly more on average, per square metre, than the latter. As at the power station the Flag Fen metalwork consists of weaponry and ornaments, most of it broken. The balance of probability now indicates that the whole of the post alignment, including the section across Flag Fen, which could be 1km (0.75mile) in total length, is likely to be a huge religious monument.

Excavation during the long, hot summer of 1990 produced solid evidence that Flag Fen and the Fengate power station are all part of the same site. First, work with tree-rings demonstrated that a high proportion of the timbers from each area were growing at the same time. Second, as we excavated down to the lowest timbers at the main Flag Fen excavation we came across a bronze stick-pin of unusual continental type; a large socketed spearhead; and, most excitingly, the lower part of a sword scabbard, known as a chape (*colour plate 28*). Like the power station finds of 1989, these were Late

67 Half an axle which had been reused as a peg to secure other timbers in the lower levels at Flag Fen. The small square hole was for the wooden lynch pin (which survived)

Bronze Age weapons or ornaments. There was nothing useful or utilitarian in this collection of metal objects. Each item had been deliberately broken, and the spearhead had been carefully hidden beneath a large, axed log.

Archaeologists have long been aware of the deliberate, 'ritual' deposition of Bronze Age metalwork in wetlands. Of course we cannot be certain that all of the many thousands of Bronze Age metalwork finds from the Fens got there during religious or sacrificial 'rituals', some might simply represent casual loss, others might have been hidden there for safety, but the sheer quantity of complete or deliberately damaged items found in the Fens is too enormous to support the idea that Bronze Age people were either absurdly forgetful or too lazy to keep track of their valuables. There is also a problem in deciding what parts of the Fen were indeed truly wet in the Bronze Age – many areas, for example, may well have been small dry islands. It is very easy when studying a region such as Fenland from outside, to treat it as all the same, whereas in reality, as we have seen, the apparently flat, featureless modern countryside hides a wealth of complex and highly diverse ancient landscapes.

So, having itemised reasons to be cautious, we are left with a core of unusual, apparently inexplicable, finds that must owe their existence in the Fen to religious or other 'rituals'. The main group of such 'ritual' finds is surely the weapons, many of which show clear signs of deliberate destruction. The huge quantities and high quality of later Bronze Age metalwork recovered from the Fens and certain rivers of southern Britain (particularly the Thames) has led archaeologists recently to draw comparisons with the rich barrow burials of the preceding Neolithic and Early Bronze Ages. Maybe, it is argued, we are seeing here symbolic, if not actual burial of important people in the waters of rivers and fens. It should also be pointed out that this is not a phenomenon restricted to Britain alone, as Bronze Age metalwork is known from wetland situations over large areas of northern and Atlantic Europe – although nowhere are the quantities as great as in southern Britain.

Although the general nature of the depositional rites in later Bronze and Iron Age Britain is similar and often involves weaponry, causeways and water, no two sites are ever identical. I will discuss the nearby site at Fiskerton shortly, but here all I need to note is that the items found there include large numbers of practical, workmanlike tools, such as axes, rasps and so forth. These seem to be largely absent at Flag Fen and suggest either that rituals changed between the Bronze and Iron Ages or, more probably, that people living in the two regions had their own ideas about religion – ideas that had developed over millennia.

The 'funerary' argument has much to recommend it, and at Flag Fen and the power station we can, I believe, argue that death featured prominently. I am sure that the smashed black shale bracelets and armlets might well have had some funerary significance. On the other hand I also think there was more to what went on at Flag Fen than merely the disposal or remembrance of the dead. For a start, thanks to metal detectors we have, for the first time, an idea of the enormous variety of metalwork that was deposited in the waters. This surely must indicate both a range of people and a range of activities.

There are magnificent items doubtless worth the modern equivalent of large sums of money and there are humbler items, maybe worth much less. The key to understanding what might have been going on lies in the broken state of so many objects. Prior to the Middle Bronze Age, grave goods in barrows often included weapons and ornaments, but they are rarely, if ever, deliberately smashed. This is something new. It may well have an underlying economic purpose. Professor Richard Bradley, for example, has suggested that some metal was being withdrawn from circulation to keep prices high, but this was probably not in the forefront of people's minds at the time. Furthermore, the destruction of something valuable in the naturally open surroundings of water is essentially a public act, and one which could be interpreted as a display of wealth and prestige.

Maybe similar ideas are applicable to Flag Fen. Perhaps the public destruction of valuable items, such as the swords, was indeed a display of wealth, power and prestige, but the vast majority of offerings were very much smaller in scale and were probably about more private rites, such as the commemoration of an ordinary family member who had recently died, been married, had given birth or had reached adulthood. These are some of the usual rites of passage, many of which could have been celebrated at Flag Fen.

I have suggested that many of the rites celebrated along the post alignment would have been small scale, perhaps family affairs, and I drew attention to the symbols of family life represented by, among other things, the four unused or only lightly used quernstones. It just so happened that these were found directly below one of the transverse 'partitions' that might possibly have subdivided the post alignment into a series of 5-6m long segments when it was first constructed. If these segments did indeed exist, they continued to be respected well into the Iron Age, because a finely decorated sword scabbard plate was found on a partition line, long after the final replacement of the last timbers. Maybe all of this is coincidence, but I wonder whether the occurrence of 'offerings' on the boundaries between different segments may not be a similar process to the deposition of significant items, such as complete pots or human skulls at the butt-ends, or terminals, of the segmented ditches of Neolithic causewayed enclosures?

I am not suggesting continuity from a site like Etton, which after all is about two millennia earlier than Flag Fen, but rather the re-emergence or 'convergent evolution' of a broadly similar idea. At Etton I have suggested that each ditch segment may have represented, symbolised or 'stood for' a family or lineage group. The item in the butt-end, at the causeway separating the ditch segment from that alongside it, would have expressed the identity of the kin group that practised their rituals there. Maybe the human skulls placed at the ditch ends, facing out towards the causeways, were indeed the heads of important ancestors? Maybe at Flag Fen the elaborately decorated scabbard plate belonged to a significant warrior who had left his mark on the family? We can only speculate, but if I am correct, it does suggest that ritual and ceremony were built in to the post alignment from its very inception.

Since I wrote the first version of this book a number of other 'Flag Fens' have been found in Britain, including examples from near Eastbourne, Caldicote in South Wales, the Trent valley and, closest of all, at Fiskerton in the Witham valley, just east of Lincoln. It now seems probable that there are several causeways in the Witham valley, including at least one of the Late Bronze Age, near the village of Washingborough. The Witham valley site which most closely resembles Flag Fen is actually Iron Age in date and is located near the village of Fiskerton. It was first investigated by Naomi Field in the 1980s and has recently been comprehensively written up by Naomi and Mike Parker Pearson.

Fiskerton, like Flag Fen, was indeed a causeway and like Flag Fen it ran from a mainland across to an 'island'. Along its course were deposited all sorts of valuable items, including the hilt of what is possibly the most lavishly decorated sword known from Iron Age Britain. There is also good evidence to suggest that the causeway was repaired in years when the moon went into total eclipse. Unlike Flag Fen (which does not seem to have favoured lunar eclipse years), the 'offerings' at Fiskerton were not smashed and included many tools and implements, as well as weapons and ornaments. So the two sites are by no means carbon copies. Having said that, they both possess important common themes, to do with water, journeys and the afterlife. What I am saying is that we are not looking here at an emerging religion or 'water cult', but rather at a series of commonly held concepts to do with identity and cosmology (or view of the world). These people were doubtless in close communication with one another, and with other communities much further away. They plainly had much in common, but they still expressed their beliefs in ways which expressed their own particular identities. Orthodoxy, be it Druidic or whatever, had yet to make its presence felt in the Fens.

One major mystery remains to be solved: why was the platform built and what took place there? All we can say at this stage is that the platform did indeed exist. We found a continuous spread of timber along the dykeside in our original investigations in 1982 and '84. Then we proved its extent both with the borehole surveys on either side of the Mustdyke and with the construction of the Mere in 1987. More recently one or two trial trenches have confirmed its existence, but none of these have penetrated below the uppermost timbers. Dendrochronology suggests that the platform and the post alignment are both contemporary and constructed together, as part of the same vast structure, but what was it built to achieve?

The short answer to that question is that we just do not know. Our first, 'Lake Village' idea plainly is well wide of the mark. Could it simply have served a practical purpose to consolidate a particularly wet area? Perhaps, but why make it so large and go to the trouble of providing a perimeter 'boardwalk'? My current 'best bet' is that the platform may possibly represent a miniature symbolic dryland within a wetland – in effect, a 'tamed' area intended for ritual purposes. If that seems a huge amount of effort for something so functionally useless, I can only point to Silbury Hill.

Could the platform at Flag Fen be an equivalent to that strange Iron Age road at Corlea in southern Ireland? The Corlea road was built of massive oak planks and it soon sunk into the bog.★ Some have suggested that this was an example of incompetence, but I don't share that view. Surely those Iron Age Irish wetlanders understood only too well how to construct a sound roadway. No, I believe they built the Corlea road deliberately to vanish into the waters. The road had taken a journey itself – perhaps to the realms of the ancestors. Who knows, but maybe the Flag Fen platform was seen as something similar?

★See *Britain BC*, pp. 380–391 (with references)

RITUAL AT THE BRONZE/IRON AGE TRANSITION

So far I have discussed a few ideas on the nature of the rites that were taking place at Flag Fen. Now I want to broaden the picture and consider why religion was so important in the Bronze and Iron Ages. I shall focus on Flag Fen, but similar rituals were taking place elsewhere, usually on or near water, from the mid-second millennium BC right up until Roman times. Indeed, I have argued in *Britain AD* that these rites continued through the Roman and well into the medieval period. It should also be borne in mind that these rituals were not confined to Britain and Ireland, but seem to have been a feature of western and central Europe too.

Older accounts of British prehistory discuss a series of invasions which brought with them a style of art and culture that was labelled 'Celtic'. It was believed that this culture began in central Europe and spread westwards, reaching Britain some time after 500 BC. Today very few prehistorians in Britain accept the idea of Celtic invasions and cite the maintenance of earlier landscapes, house styles, burial rites, pottery and so forth as evidence for continuity. That, of course, is not to deny that there was contact and trade with the continental mainland, which was the mechanism whereby new styles of art and other innovations came and went from Britain.

One of the aspects of the rituals practised at Flag Fen that struck me very forcibly, as the first metalwork was being revealed at the power station by the metal-detectorists, was that although the shape of the artefacts changed through time, the way that they had been treated and the items themselves remained much the same. So what we were looking at was a very conservative set of rituals which involved a dynamic, changing metal 'industry'. Take swords as an example. The earliest swords date to the middle Bronze Age, around 1300 BC, and have long thrusting blades. They were bent and broken and rivets were detached (presumably as the hilt was smashed), before being placed in the water. By the Late Bronze Age, around 900 BC, the style of swords changed from thrusting rapiers to slashing weapons where the main weight of the leaf-shaped blade was towards the tip. These weapons had more in common with a cutlass or scimitar than a rapier. But they were broken, bent and damaged before being dropped in the water and there is evidence, too, that their scabbards were mistreated as well.

The same patterns can still be recognised in the Iron Age (after 500 BC) when iron swords of so-called La Tène type were also broken before deposition although, because the iron was subject to severe corrosion, it is difficult to be precise about the extent to which they were actually smashed about. Some bronze Iron Age brooches had, however, been extensively damaged, just like earlier, Bronze Age, examples. There are other instances which illustrate the continuity and conservatism of the rituals involved at Flag Fen, but we lack the space to discuss them now.

Plainly such continuity of ritual practice argues strongly against any idea of Celtic mass-migration in the early Iron Age, but I believe there is far more to it than just that. It was Richard Bradley who first suggested the idea that the conservatism of ritual practice, that is so frequently observed in archaeology, reflects a need that people have for stability. This requirement becomes more necessary in times of social stress. Maybe we can attribute the rise of religious conservatism and fundamentalism in both America and the Middle East to such a cause. I think it very likely that the early first millennium BC was a stressful epoch. Populations were growing with some rapidity and societies were becoming increasingly hierarchical with powerful ruling elites beginning to emerge. Iron Age or 'Celtic' cultures are often described as being warrior based or 'heroic'. These social changes are reflected archaeologically by increasingly rich burials – often in carts or 'chariots' – and the appearance of hillforts. The new Iron Age villages or nucleated settlements at Fengate are further examples of these widespread social changes.

So perhaps we can see the continuance of deliberately conservative religious rituals at Flag Fen, during the latter part of the Bronze Age and the entire Iron Age, as a way of coping with social change. Of course at a place like Flag Fen, where water featured so prominently, the increasing wetness of the Iron Age Fens would have been an additional cause for concern, which again could be addressed and dealt with emotionally, if not practically, by rituals associated with water. I find it therefore unsurprising that, even though the replacement and maintenance of the timbers of the post alignment had to be abandoned around 900 BC, people continued to make offerings, and often very valuable ones, to the waters for the remainder of the millennium. Far from being idle gestures, akin to tossing small change into a fountain, the objects in the waters at Flag Fen played a major part in holding society together.

6

The Iron Age
(700 BC–AD 43)

Our story is drawing to a close, and for the first time we begin to see glimpses of a more familiar world. In many respects the countryside of Iron Age Britain was similar to that of post-Roman England, with small villages and scattered farmsteads. True, the radiating pattern of formal Roman roads was not yet in existence, but the less formal network of roads and tracks that did exist was perfectly adequate. We know for a fact that Iron Age communities in southern Britain were actively in touch with one another, and often over significant distances. It would not surprise me to learn that people living in the Peterborough area had friends and relatives who farmed in the Thames valley. The two regions are linked by the Nene valley and the natural communication routes through what is now Northamptonshire. Contact with communities further north and south would have been along the Fen margins of Lincolnshire and Cambridgeshire, respectively.

One of the most remarkable aspects of Flag Fen is that metalwork continued to be deposited in and around the posts for several centuries after the last episode of rebuilding. This would suggest that even though we know that conditions in the Early Iron Age were growing wetter, the post alignment continues to be used as a causeway, presumably during the drier months of summer. Maybe, too, the site could have been visited by boat in the winter. Although most of the metalwork belongs to the Wilburton tradition of the Late Bronze Age, a significant amount of material, including such large items as swords, continued to be deposited in the subsequent Ewart Park (mid-tenth – eighth centuries BC) and Llyn Fawr (seventh century BC) phases. There are about 20 true Iron Age metal finds including no less than two broken iron swords, the decorated bronze scabbard plate, an extraordinarily elaborate bronze plate brooch, numerous dress pins and the well-known shears in their wooden box. This is not a bad haul for a supposedly Bronze Age site!

The Iron Age landscape of lowland eastern England is characterised by small farmsteads and hamlets set in ditched and hedged fields and pastures, which are often linked together by droveways and tracks. There would have been far more woodland then than now, but otherwise the landscape bore at least a passing resemblance to that of today. But there were some major social and technological changes in the earlier first millennium BC. Apart from the introduction of iron we see the appearance of a new, improved wheat, known as spelt, the appearance of villages, rather than dispersed farmsteads and the widespread, if uneven, switch from a livestock-based economy to a newer style of so-called 'mixed farming', where livestock and arable both featured prominently. I shall have more to say about some of these things shortly, but here I want simply to stress that the new was not necessarily 'better' than the old. The Iron Age followed the Bronze Age, it did not surpass it.

Any view of prehistory inevitably tends to stress how technology, culture and society are progressively evolving. We start in caves wearing skins, acquire metalwork, horses, chariots, steam engines, cars and ultimately spaceships. Meanwhile society progresses from barbarism to modern democracy, with a few hiccups in the Middle Ages. I find this view of the world profoundly flawed, largely because it is so mechanistic. It denies individuals what today we would refer to as their human rights – to be themselves. Archaeology and anthropology show that while technology might improve as populations increase, this does not necessarily amount to 'progress'. Who would say, for example, that we in the West live better, more rewarding lives than, say the Bushmen of the Kalahari Desert just 50 years ago?

The people of every archaeological period, lived their lives very much influenced by their own history, just as we do today. Their ideas of time were undoubtedly more cyclical or seasonal than ours today, but by the Iron Age people in southern Britain had been living within an organised, managed and partitioned countryside for at least 3,500 years. In that time they must have developed a view of their own past which must have played a major role in shaping their actions. It is these histories that we as prehistorians can never recover, although we can obtain glimpses of what they might have included when we read, for example, the heroic poems of the Ulster Cycle, which most scholars agree have roots in pre-Christian Ireland. But the fact remains that we have no knowledge of the lore and legends that motivated and structured the lives of people in the Bronze or Iron Ages. After all, it is the possession of history that makes us human.

Given this huge void in our understanding, we must beware of assuming that they must always have acted like us, only more ancient. 2,500 years is a very long time indeed, and I suspect we would find life in the Iron Age far stranger than just living in a round-house and eating off coarse pottery. I am convinced we would find that their whole system of beliefs, standards and values was based on a view of history that was entirely alien to us. So this is probably an appropriate place to say a few words about our own attempts to recreate the past experimentally. I should add here that these attempts are to do with technology alone; they cannot address the really important questions, like why certain tasks were done, or what motivated people do them.

In chapter 4 I described how we recreated a Bronze Age round-house within its original fields, but this was only an 'experiment' insofar as the roof was concerned; the rest was fairly straightforward and was based on pioneering work by the late Peter Reynolds at the Little Butser experimental Iron Age farm, near Petersfield in Hampshire. Having said that, I personally have quite serious qualms about some of the constructional techniques we employed: I find it hard to believe, knowing what I do about the sophistication of prehistoric carpentry, for example, that so much use was made of crude lashing. Prehistoric sites rarely produce evidence for twine or cordage, and yet our reconstructed buildings used it extensively. We do our best, but the most we can hope to achieve is just a very crude approximation of what might have existed in the past.

The Bronze Age building presented more technical problems than the Iron Age building we erected in 1990. This particular house was based on one found in the Cat's Water settlement (to be described below). The building enclosed an area 10m (33ft) in diameter and the apex of the roof was 6m (18ft) above the ground (68). We decided not to finish it properly, using thatch, sedge and daub, but instead roofed it with a synthetic material that allows one to appreciate the complexities of even our imperfect carpentry (69).

The synthetic roof lasted ten years, but was ripped apart by a storm. We decided to replace it with a more authentic thatched roof, using second-hand wheat straw and reed (new wheat straw was prohibitively expensive). This new roof has stood up well, but we decided to add a porch to exclude the worst of the Fen gales (70). I can only conclude from this that the original Cat's Water Iron Age settlement must have been far more protected by trees than the open arable fields of modern Flag Fen. We have decided not to daub the walls, both to show their wattle work structure and to let in more light. In cold winters we line the walls with straw bales.

Some experimenters have attempted to work out the man hours that might have been spent erecting prehistoric houses, Stonehenge, or whatever. These worthy attempts are doomed to failure because they ignore the many thousands of years cumulative experience that the ancient craftsmen could have drawn upon. They also assume that people *wanted* to build efficiently, in a cost-effective way. This way of looking at the past assumes that Iron Age communities thought like modern western industrialists. But maybe their history had taught them to do certain tasks in other, less efficient ways: it could, for example, have been more important to gather a large number of people together than to carry out a particular job in the shortest possible time.

The archaeological record of the Iron Age is marked by a sharp increase in the quantity of pottery found on excavations. By this period people were beginning to understand far better how to control and use fire. Iron smelting (the actual extraction of the metal from the ore) required sustained high temperatures and

68 Work starts of the reconstruction of an Iron Age round house in the Flag Fen archaeological park, June 1990. Note the steeper roof angle needed for a thatched roof (compare with *colour plate 8*). In the foreground are some of the oak timbers that were split experimentally the previous season

69 The Iron Age round-house with its fitted synthetic roof, July 1990. The visitors are walking along the Roman road

a degree of control that is hard to replicate experimentally today, unless one has a good knowledge of metallurgy. This greater understanding of pyrotechnology was not confined to the metalworkers and smiths alone, for pottery improves by leaps and bounds by the end of the Middle Iron Age, around 200 BC. Not only are the ceramics better fired and harder, but they were produced in much greater quantities. The next technological breakthrough, the introduction of the potter's wheel, took place in the Late Iron Age, towards the end of the first century BC.

These technological improvements have tended to distort the archaeological record. If one takes the area around Peterborough there are truly gigantic quantities of locally produced Roman wares, large quantities of Iron Age pottery, but Bronze Age and Neolithic potsherds are more lightly fired and do not survive in the topsoil for very long, especially when subjected to modern farming methods. This tends to give a false impression. It is possible that the population rose in early Roman times, but not by a quantum leap. Similarly I would suggest that the Late Bronze Age population was every bit as large, if not actually greater than that of the earliest Iron Age. It was not until the Middle Iron Age, around say 350 BC that the local population began, quite dramatically to increase. So one must beware of leaping to false conclusions on the basis of archaeological finds alone.

70 The synthetic roof of the Iron Age round-house lasted ten years, before it was ripped apart in a gale. This thatched replacement was added in the summer of 2000

THE IRON AGE AT FENGATE

Iron Age settlement at Fengate between 500 and 300 BC was confined to two main areas. The first is much closer to Peterborough than the sites I investigated in the 1970s and '80s and was revealed by Wyman Abbott before the Second World War. It consisted of a number of deep pits which contained large quantities of Early Iron Age pottery, now in Peterborough Museum. These pits were once thought to have been individually filled in one operation, but as we saw in chapter 2, this was probably not the case. Other than that rather negative comment, it is difficult to say anything intelligent about this site.

That paragraph is pretty much what I wrote in the first version of this book. Since then there has been further work, undertaken by the Cambridge University Unit, as part of their commercial operation. The site in question is known as the Tower Works and it consists of what town planners today call a 'brownfield' site. The first time I visited the site, I think it was in February 1997, I remember being deafened by the noise of a digger-mounted Kango hammer drilling its percussive way through solid concrete floors. Happily this concrete had barely any foundations and actually preserved the archaeological remains beneath it very well. I very much doubt whether survival would have been as good in an average modern arable field.

We expected most of the site to have been destroyed by a combination of nineteenth- and early twentieth-century hand-dug gravel pits and pre-Second World War industrial development, but to everyone's amazement that hadn't happened. Instead the Cambridge team found evidence for Bronze Age fields, which extended the known system 400-500m to the south. In addition they found filled pits and post-holes associated with a substantial rectangular building, which the Iron Age specialist J.D. Hill (now at The British Museum) dated to about 900-700 BC, which is technically-speaking in the Late Bronze Age. It's hard to be certain about the rectangular building and the pits, but they must, surely, represent the remains of a far more substantial settlement than the small farmsteads that were scattered throughout the main Fengate Bronze Age fields. I suspect that we are looking here at the origins of the village-like or nucleated settlements that are such an important aspect of the local Iron Age settlement pattern. So far there are no reasons to believe that the Tower Works settlement was ever defended by a large ditch or bank.

The second site was located further inland, on the Vicarage Farm sub-site. The subsoil was Cornbrash, a type of crumbly limestone, which had been quite severely eroded by ploughing, so that all of the very shallow archaeological evidence had been destroyed. This probably explains the absence of house foundations and other slight features, such as stake- and post-holes. The commonest features were pits, some of them deep enough to be 'sock' wells and many had pottery thrown into them; in this respect the Vicarage Farm settlement resembled that discovered by Abbott just before the First World War. Some of the pottery was rather remarkable, including a unique sherd with chalky inlaid decoration, and another with a finely made, wrapped wooden handle, for all the world like a Victorian teapot!

The pits and hollows of the Vicarage Farm settlement were grouped together, which suggests that they once belonged to a farmstead or small hamlet and there was some evidence for 'settlement drift', whereby the community gradually moved across the land, perhaps covering 100m in two or three centuries. Assuming that it really was 'settlement drift', and not the chance relocation of several intermittent, short-lived settlements, then it was hardly rapid. Again, although we were not able to find the foundations of any actual buildings the concentration of pits and wells suggests that this, too, was an undefended nucleated settlement.

The principal Iron Age settlement was located on the Cat's Water sub-site, much nearer the edges of the fen and just 300m south-west of the power station post alignment's landfall (*colour plate 29*). Its discovery, although slightly less dramatic than Flag Fen, is also of some interest. Again, 'luck' was on our side.

The well-known aerial photograph of Fengate, published in the Royal Commission 'Peterborough Volume', shows two droveway ditches running diagonally across the picture, from east to west. The droveway, which was much larger than the Bronze Age ones and must have been intended for the herding of really quite large herds, ended in a series of ditched farmyards. A scatter of locally-made Roman pottery on the field surface above these ditched yards strongly suggested the presence of a Romano-British farm there. So when we started to excavate them in 1975, we thought things were going to be straight-forward enough.

It was at about this time that Dr Paul Craddock of the British Museum Research Laboratory first contacted us for a suitable site to test his soil phosphate analyses. We have seen how successful they were on Bronze Age droveways, but we also wanted to see how well they worked in an actual farmyard, where phosphate concentrations were likely to be very much higher. The Cat's Water site seemed ideal, as it looked so simple: we would be able to get a clear, single-period picture without 'background noise' and other interference caused by later or earlier activity in the same area. It would provide an excellent test case for Paul's method. At least, that is what we fondly hoped.

Dr Craddock arrived with a team of trainees from a local detention centre. The work was hard, as each sample involved hand-drilling through stiff clay, and the conditions were pretty unpleasant, but Paul and his team did a splendid job. When the analyses were plotted out, to our amazement the area of highest phosphate was outside the ditched farmyards. This seemed to make no sense whatsoever, but the results were very definite and could not be shrugged off.

I then retrieved as many air photos as I could find and took a much closer look at the land immediately north of the ditched yards. With the eye of faith I could just make out one or two faint, ghost-like ditches, which we now know were lying, partially obscured, beneath third-century AD Roman flood clay. I am quite convinced that we would have missed them entirely had Paul Craddock and his team not done their work.

So we started our excavation well to the north of the main yards, on the off-chance that the phosphate tests and faint cropmarks would tell an interesting story. The overburden was thick and difficult to machine, especially when wet, so we had to resort to heavy-duty equipment – motorway scrapers with bulldozer assistance – and I was very concerned lest we might cause damage. However, we were able to use more gentle machines once the stiff flood clay had been removed, and there, just a little below the clay, were the remains of a buried Iron Age hamlet. It was this settlement, and not the few ditches that showed up through the flood clay on the air photo, which had raised the soil phosphate levels. And there was little wonder that they were so phosphate-rich, for there was archaeology everywhere. I had never seen so many pits, post-holes, gullies and ditches, all of which showed up as dark marks in the exposed subsoil.

Following the success of the phosphate survey, we arranged with the detention centre for a party of six to eight trainees to come and dig. In addition to the actual trainees, there were supervisory staff such as minibus drivers, all of whom joined in; in effect, it meant that we had at our disposal an extra 10-12 excavators – approximately double our regular workforce. This influx of new people saved the day, because we now had one team of a dozen working on the Bronze Age ditched fields, and another of the same size (or very slightly larger) working at Cat's Water, where the quantities of finds and features threatened to engulf us.

Although not paid for by a developer, as would be the case today, these were still 'rescue' excavations carried out to very tight budgets. Our deadlines too were real. Factories now stand where once we had been digging, and the pressure was all-pervasive. Everyone was in a state of collapse at the end of each day. We knew we had a big challenge on our hands when we were confronted by what we thought would be a straightforward Romano-British farm, but Paul's phosphate survey hinted at something altogether larger – and older. I felt it in my bones: we were going to be very stretched.

The Fengate Cat's Water Iron Age settlement was dug between 1975 and 1978. It consisted of about 55 buildings in all, of which about ten would have been in use at the same time. Of these ten buildings, five were for people, and five for livestock. The floor area of the houses would not have been large enough to have accommodated more than a single, or nuclear, family consisting of parents and their children, so we must imagine a small hamlet of five houses and perhaps 30 people in all. The houses were grouped quite tightly together, and the whole settlement – houses, barns, animal byres, ditches and yards – did not occupy much more than a hectare (2.5 acres) of land (71).

The houses were round, walled in woven wattle and plastered with 'daub' – clay mixed with chopped straw or cow dung (72). Sometimes we found direct evidence for the walling; in one or two cases buildings, or parts of buildings, had caught fire and the daub had become fired, rather like pottery. Its self-firing was fuelled by the wattle and the chopped straw mixed in it; after it had been fired it retained its shape, with the wattlework impressions clearly visible.

Unlike the round-houses of the Bronze Age, the Iron Age structures on Cat's Water were probably thatched with local reed, rather then straw. Reed grows everywhere in the Fens. It's a superb thatching material, shedding water better than straw and lasting very much longer We found the foundations of several dozen round, thatched buildings, but never any evidence for the stout internal posts required to support a turf roof. So did this mean that Iron Age houses were thatched? I think so, although it has been suggested that the internal roof-support posts need not have been sunk into the ground, since they were only carrying a vertical load and were not subject to any sideways forces. It has also been argued that the ground water-table (which we know was high in the Late Iron Age) would soon have rotted the posts; so it would be sensible not to sink them unless it was absolutely necessary.

71 The Fengate Cat's Water Iron Age settlement during excavation in 1976. The ditched yard in the foreground surrounded a round-house. The circular eaves-drip gullies surrounding other round-houses can be seen in the background

I have subsequently constructed three round-houses, two with, and one without roof-support posts, and I am convinced that internal posts must be earth fast and not free-standing, particularly when several people are scrambling around on the roof, laying or repairing turf or thatch. Furthermore if these buildings were used as animal byres, as seems highly probable, a ram, cow or pig with an itch would soon topple any free-standing post. No, I think we have evidence in these house plans for an important change in roof construction: a shift from turf and thatch to thatch on its own.

Burnt mud walls and pottery were not the only items in fired clay to be found: we also recovered many triangular weights, weighing, when complete, about 1kg (2.25lbs) each. There is some doubt about the function of these weights, which are usually perforated at the corners; some archaeologists would interpret them as thatch weights, or net sinkers, but these explanations are somewhat impractical: logs or rocks make the best thatch weights (which have to be very heavy, as anyone who has ever sheeted a haystack in a gale will tell you), and stones make the best net sinkers, as water will soon penetrate and weaken such poorly fired clay. The most reasonable explanation is that these weights were used in looms, to provide tension for the vertical threads, or warps.

72 A house within the Fengate Cat's Water Iron Age settlement. The deeper curving gully in the foreground ran around the outside of the building and took run-off from the roof. The shallower gully running concentrically within it was the wall foundation trench. The figure is standing on the edge of an earlier 'sock' well that had been filled-in when the house was built

Every Iron Age settlement site produces a mass of fired clay, and frequently it is impossible to decide on its original use – if any. But at Fengate we were fortunate to have better than usual preservation and most objects were found in the ground more or less where they had been dropped, or placed, in antiquity. We were able to reassemble one large mass of fired clay lumps and chunks into a flued oven, with a central fire-hole, a lower storey fire-box and an upper storey oven, which was given additional heat by a number of smaller fire-holes or perforations through the oven floor. It was a sophisticated and well thought-out structure.

The ditched fields and droveways of the Bronze Age had been abandoned for about 700 years when the Cat's Water settlement was first built, somewhere around 300 BC. The earlier banks and ditches must have been faintly, if at all, visible and the only trace of the previous landscape might have been an occasional huge oak tree that survived in an out-of-the-way hedge. Charles French analysed the snails in the bottom of Iron Age ditches at Cat's Water and showed them to be species that liked conditions very much wetter than their Bronze Age antecedents. So we must picture these ditches lined with reeds and probably choked with sedge and pondweed.

We have seen that the Bronze Age way of life was based on livestock with droveways running down to the Fen; people lived in single family settlements dotted around their fields. The later Iron Age hamlet at Cat's Water could not be more different. If anything, its yards faced away from the Fen and its ditches disregarded the arrangement of the earlier landscape. In many respects the change of landscape 'style' between the Bronze and Iron Ages was greater than that between the earliest Neolithic and the Bronze Age proper, discussed in chapters 3 and 4. As I have already suggested, this change of landscape mirrored a change in the local economy away from livestock, to a more balanced pattern of mixed farming, which could better support a larger population.

Iron Age villagers at Cat's Water grew wheat and barley on the higher, flood-free land back from the Fen – most probably around the land now occupied by Perkins Engines' enormous diesel-engine factory, north and west of the Vicarage Farm sub-site. There is not much direct evidence for cereals – a few grains and fragments of chaff – but this is not altogether surprising, given the Cat's Water settlement's very low-lying position. Wheat and barley do not tolerate being flooded during their growing season, and as the Iron Age Fenland was very wet, this might well account for the rarity of hard evidence. We did, however, discover numerous sherds of large vessels that are generally thought to be grain storage jars, and the eaves-drip gully of one round-house produced a near-complete quernstone (millstone), made from Lincolnshire limestone.

A recent commercial excavation, this time by a team from Birmingham University, revealed evidence for spelt wheat from a later Bronze Age pit just above the flood-free zone at the edge of the fen, down towards the Tower Works site. This was a very early example of the improved new wheat and it suggests that the transition to a more mixed style of farming was already underway towards the end of the Bronze Age. One could argue long and hard whether this change was primarily a response to increasing wetness or growing population, or indeed both, but I am now increasingly of the opinion that it was a gradual process.

Apart from cereals, the inhabitants of Iron Age Fengate grew apples (pips were found), and vegetables probably included celery, mustard leaves and parsnips; thyme might have been used as a strewing or culinary herb. I use the word 'probably' because it is very hard indeed to distinguish early cultivars from wild species – and it is possible that unimproved wild species were actually grown. The main weed of modern sugar beet fields, for example, is fat hen or *Chenopodium album*. This plant was found in archaeological features at Cat's Water and makes a very palatable green vegetable, when cooked like spinach (I prefer it pressed quite dry and with plenty of salt and butter).

The meadows of the Fen-edge around the Cat's Water settlement would have provided grazing for cattle, sheep, goats and pigs. After about 500-300 BC conditions out in the Flag Fen basin were becoming very much wetter and much of the grazing would have vanished under water, although the drier fringes could still have supported meadows. Liver fluke, which saps the vigour of sheep, would have been an increasing problem in wetter times, but foot rot, which came to Britain from Australia in the nineteenth century, would not. Instead sheep farmers would have had to contend with the less serious cause of limping, known as scald.

Some wild animals were still hunted – a few deer, for example – and fishing also took place (numerous large pike jaw bones were found during the excavations at Cat's Water and Flag Fen). I suspect, however, that the available archaeological evidence tends to underestimate the importance of fish in the Iron Age and earlier prehistoric diet. The problem of finding archaeological evidence for fishing illustrates the problems of interpreting bone evidence in general: we have to assume that the material we find on site is broadly speaking representative of what took place there in the past. Sometimes this may not be a correct assumption to make, because rotting fish remains stink, attract flies and are generally unpleasant. They are quite easy to dispose of in water, under a scoop of sand, in pig feed, or whatever. The bones themselves are generally small and do not survive particularly well, especially on sites with acid soils.

I therefore think it very significant that Iron Age drainage ditches of the Cat's Water settlement produced 34 bones or fragments of pike, 9 of tench and 31 of bream. Incidentally, these fish could not have died in the ditches, where they lived, unaffected by man, for the simple reason that they were never represented by complete skeletons, but just by single loose bones. This suggests that they were discarded with other household rubbish. A total of around 80 bones is hardly a huge collection, but I think it a significant one. I cannot believe that a settlement located on the very edge of the Fens, at one of the wettest periods in their history, could have ignored such a vitally important source of winter protein. I can't prove it, but I would not be surprised if during the winter the Iron Age villagers of Cat's Water caught fish and eels by the hundredweight.

Prehistoric Fengate must have been an ornithologist's dream. The Iron Age and Roman deposits at Cat's Water produced bones of the following: goose, mallard, pelican, cormorant, heron, stork, mute swan, barnacle goose, teal, tableduck, merganser, sea eagle, goshawk, hawk, buzzard, crane, coot and crow (two species). Most were probably eaten, since they are represented, like the fish, by loose bones amongst the domestic refuse.

It would appear that in the later Iron Age Fen people ate a diet that was not radically unlike that of pre-drainage days, around 400 years ago. But there were other products of the wetland that folk also could use: willow bark, for example, could be boiled up to make a rather soporific, pain-relieving aspirin 'tea'. However there is also evidence for other medicines: seeds of opium poppy were found in late Iron Age or early Roman soils in one of the settlement's ditches. Opium-derived medicines were traditionally used in the Fens to relieve the pains of malaria which was endemic until very recently. Incidentally, in the English climate the sap of opium poppies produces an analgesic or pain-relieving, rather than a powerful hallucinogenic drug.

So to sum up, although the Cat's Water settlement was positioned at the edge of the true wetland, it would still have been very damp by modern standards, and this we have tried to show in the excellent model that was made shortly after the site's excavation in 1978. The model, which can be seen in Peterborough Museum, shows a small part of the Late Iron Age settlement.

The people who lived at Cat's Water, like many other Iron Age communities in Britain did not dispose of their dead in a very archaeologically-visible fashion: for example, there seems to have been no formally-defined cemetery area. Or perhaps more likely we have yet to find one. Instead human remains were found buried in various places through the settlement. The body of a child was buried in the crouched position in a house eaves-drip gully; the other five intact burials were all crammed into small pit-like graves, tightly crouched up; one was even squeezed into a sack or bag (*73* and *74*). All were either teenagers or young adults in their twenties.

73 A partially disarticulated burial from the Fengate Cat's Water Iron Age settlement. This skeleton of a young person had been squeezed into a tiny grave

74 A so-called 'bag burial' from the Fengate Cat's Water Iron Age settlement. The bones are disarticulated and their arrangement in the ground suggests that they were placed in a bag before burial in a shallow grave

Three cremations, in small pits, were also recovered. This rather sad catalogue of burials is greatly increased if we take into account finds of loose human bones which were found mixed in with animal bones, pottery and general debris from pits, ditches and other settlement features of the hamlet. It is hard to interpret these loose bones: some could derive from graves that had been disturbed, but they are so commonly encountered on settlement sites of the Iron Age in Britain that some kind of 'exposure' or excarnation burial has been suggested. Perhaps a body was placed on a platform, rather than in the ground, and when the flesh had rotted, or been removed by carrion crows, the bones were no longer considered to have any particular significance. The person's soul had flown off with the birds.

But whatever happened, a significant number of bodies had to have been disposed of somehow. Even if only 30 people occupied the site at any one time, that would still give us a total population of several hundred individuals over the 300 or so years that the settlement was inhabited. If these people had all been given exposure 'burial' within or near to the settlement, then one would expect to have found more than the 20 pieces and fragments of human bone that we sorted out from among the huge collection of animal bones. I suspect the majority of the adult dead were buried away from the settlement, either alone, or in unmarked cemeteries – perhaps out in Flag Fen somewhere?

THE COMING OF THE ROMANS

The final episode of our story can be briefly stated. The Roman military authorities took a road from the then small market town at *Durobrivae* (on the A1 west of Peterborough, near the village of Water Newton), ran it across the land where Peterborough now stands, and over to the Fen-edge in Fengate. They then 'island hopped' the road from Fengate to Northey and Whittlesey, Coates and March, ultimately leaving the wetlands at the Norfolk fen-edge town of Denver, at which point the road, known today as the Fen Causeway joins up with the larger Norfolk system of Roman roads. The Fen Causeway is widely thought to have been built as part of the crushing of Boudica's revolt of AD 60/61, and whether this is true or not, it was certainly built sometime in the later first century AD.

One might have expected the presence of an important road a few metres to the north to have had some effect on the Cat's Water settlement, but apparently it did not. There is no sign of a roadside inn, known as a mansio, nor is there a sudden increase in prosperity. One might have expected some roadside 'ribbon development', but this does not seem to have happened. Although doubtless they used the road as a way of taking goods to the market in *Durobrivae*, for some reason the inhabitants of the Cat's Water hamlet chose to ignore the Fen Causeway. I still find that very odd.

The Cat's Water settlement continued into Roman times until the third century AD, when widespread freshwater flooding throughout the southern Fenlands caused people to seek higher and safer ground. Happily for the survival of the buried archaeological remains, people stayed clear of the area until recent times when we, in our infinite wisdom, have seen fit to drain and develop the land.

THE DEATH OF THE LANDSCAPE

When I wrote the first version of this book I concluded with a Postscript which ended with the words: '... no archaeological book is ever the final word, just as no archaeological interpretation is ever correct. In the final analysis, archaeology is a humanity and archaeologists, alas, are only too human.' Oh well, a little pious perhaps and certainly wide of the mark as regards my humanity, but what worries me is the implication that somehow people will be able to go back to the Fengate landscape and reassess what I have written. The reason that worries me is that the raw material for future study is vanishing before our eyes, not just through drainage, but through destruction brought about by industrial development. As archaeologists many of us have grown to live with this process – indeed it pays us a not-always-very-good living. But it does at least pay something.

I used to drive to Flag Fen along the Fengate fen margins. In the 1980s there were still fields along the road. Now I think there is just one left. Pretty much the whole of the southern part of Fengate has been built over. True, Ben Robinson, the first-rate archaeological curator employed by the City Council, has done wonders to insist on good quality excavation, but he has neither the power, nor the authority to stop development in order to preserve a typical slice of this landscape for posterity. Certainly, if there was an intact burial mound, or some such, he could have it scheduled for the future, but something as seemingly humdrum as some Bronze Age field ditches, or an Iron Age settlement cannot be regarded as of potential national significance – the usual test for the creation of a Scheduled Ancient Monument.

One aspect of this destruction that I find particularly depressing concerns the loss of wet deposits. As archaeologists we deplore the fact that wooden artefacts simply disintegrate on exposure to dry air, but there is so much more to it than that. Wetland deposits contain such an extraordinary wealth of information. Perhaps I can illustrate this by reproducing a slide that was given to me in 1992 by Maisie Taylor. It shows some of the tiny items that can be sieved from two small samples of peaty soil from Flag Fen (75). Dry them out and they soon vanish.

My original idea, expressed in this book's sub-title, was to discuss the Death of the Landscape. I was going to talk about later Roman flooding, subsequent alluviation and the absence of Saxon period finds in Fengate. Then I had second thoughts. After all, wetness is just that: it is not death, and an inundated landscape is not a dead landscape. On the other hand, I would suggest that an urban fringe, post-modern industrial suburb is as close to wasteland as I ever want to find myself. For me at least, it is spiritually and culturally dead. So I want to finish this book with some thoughts on the nature of landscape death.

I find it increasingly hard to come to terms with the rapidity of the archaeological destruction that is happening every day in the early twenty-first century. Such development is often welcomed by archaeologists because it provides them with work. Meanwhile, while they allow destruction ahead of development, members of my profession have developed a dislike for 'research' excavation, which is often seen as unnecessary. Personally I would ten times rather take part in an under-funded, but well thought-out piece of research digging than return to the competitive world of rescue archaeology, where the meaning and context of what has been revealed is rarely given adequate attention. I did not become an archaeologist simply to dig remains out of the ground, for money, like so many potatoes.

There are a few flickers of hope. For example, Ben Robinson has deliberately positioned some of the huge concrete floors of new factories and warehouses

75 A photograph showing bark, twigs and small woodchips sieved from just two small samples of peaty soil from Flag Fen. *Photo by Derek Rootes*

over sensitive archaeological deposits, in the hope that archaeologists in the future could replicate what the Cambridge University team achieved so successfully at the Tower Works site. But it will undoubtedly require more data, dug moreover to a higher standard, if people in the future are to reinterpret what we have revealed about Fengate, Flag Fen and Northey in the last 30 years of the twentieth century and first ten of the twenty-first. Can, or will such information survive, given the current pace of development in eastern England? Perhaps it will, for a few decades anyhow. What worries me is this: in another 15 years will anyone (and it won't be me!) be in a position to do a third major rewrite of this book? Yes, is the short answer, given the exciting new discoveries at Bradley Fen (*colour plate 30*) and elsewhere, but I am convinced that a fourth rewrite in 30 years' time cannot happen, quite simply because the data will be gone. That really will prove to be the end of the story – and with it the true death of the archaeological landscape.

Appendix:
Planning a visit
to Flag Fen

Further Reading

Glossary

Index

Appendix: Planning a visit to Flag Fen

There is much to see at Flag Fen and we normally recommend that visitors allow themselves at least half a day for a visit. The site is located in Peterborough's Eastern Industrial Area Ordnance Survey Map 142, Grid Reference TL227989. There are some six other Flag Fens in Fenland, including one at Whittlesey which appears prominently on Ordnance Survey Maps. So do not be misled! The site is clearly signed from the Peterborough ring-road (A1139). Flag Fen is open to the public every day of the year, except between 24 December and 2 January. The usual opening hours are from 10.00am, last admissions 4.00pm, closed at 5.00pm, but seasonal variations apply (we suggest you check our website or telephone if in any doubt). There is a book and gift shop, also a cafeteria in the visitor centre. For further information (including admission prices) write to:

Flag Fen Bronze Age Centre
The Droveway
Northey Road
Peterborough PE6 7QJ.
Tel: 01733 313414
Fax: 01733 349957
Email: office@flagfen.com
Website: www.flagfen.com

OTHER PLACES IN PETERBOROUGH WELL WORTH A VISIT

Peterborough has three heritage attractions of national importance within the City limits: Flag Fen, the Cathedral and Longthorpe Tower. The first two are open on weekends. Longthorpe Tower is more problematic and we strongly advise potential visitors to make arrangements in advance of their visit. The city also possesses a first-rate museum. With the museum, Flag Fen, the Cathedral, plus walks and visits to other attractions (for example, the church of St Kynburga at Castor, dedicated in 1124, is one of the finest Norman churches in England), the City of Peterborough will give visitors interested in history and archaeology an excellent weekend away from home. For details on accommodation, places to eat etc. contact the Tourist Information Centre on (Tel) 01733 452336 or (Email) tic@peterborough.gov.uk

Peterborough Museum and Art Gallery
Priestgate
Peterborough
PE1 1LF; Tel: 01733-343329
Email: museum@peterborough.gov.uk
Website: www.peterboroughheritage.org.uk

Peterborough Museum contains a fine collection of prehistoric material from Fengate, including most of the pre-War finds of George Wyman Abbott and the archive of the 1970s excavations. It has a fine collection of Romano-British material, including replicas of the Water Newton treasure (the earliest Christian church plate from Britain). The Museum is particularly notable for its large collection of bone carvings made by Napoleonic prisoners-of-war from the Norman Cross POW camp, just outside the modern city. Peterborough was the home of the inventor of the efficient modern diesel engine, Sir Frank Perkins, whose company Perkins Engines, still has a large factory near Fengate. The Museum has a fine display of Industrial archaeology and engineering history. The area is also well known to fossil enthusiasts and there is a fine display of palaeontology and geology.

Peterborough Cathedral

Tel: 01733 343342; Website: www.peterborough-cathedral.co.uk
Probably the least-known of Britain's great ancient cathedrals. The standing structure is mainly Norman, and is largely unspoilt. It also possesses a unique, triple arcaded Early English west front. The interior is internationally famous for the Romanesque painted nave ceiling (about 1220). It consists of diamond-shaped panels which depict saints, bishops, animals and other images illustrating the central theme: 'the powers through which God created and rules the world'.* It is unique, being the earliest and by far the largest painted medieval ceiling in Europe north of the Alps (the painted ceilings at Ely and Waltham Abbey are both nineteenth-century). Canterbury and Norwich possessed ceilings comparable with Peterborough, but both were destroyed by fire in the Middle Ages. Peterborough's ceiling was recently affected by fire, but mercifully the damage has proved to be superficial. The interior is also unspoiled by too keen restoration or an over-profusion of memorials, largely due to destruction in the Civil War. Henry VIII ordered that Katharine of Aragon's body be buried in Peterborough after her death in 1536, following her imprisonment in Kimbolton Castle. The standard of Henry VIII over her tomb was given by the present Queen. Unmissable.

Longthorpe Tower

The site is in the care of English Heritage and is open from 1 April to 30 September. Currently visits are for pre-booked groups only. If sufficient people phone up we might be able to change this unfortunate state of affairs. For details of opening hours and admission prices, phone English Heritage at 01223 582700 or 0845 3010006, Website: www.english-heritage.org.uk. Ordnance Survey Grid Reference (map 142): TL163983). Longthorpe Tower is in Longthorpe on the old A47 3km (2 miles) west of the city centre.

Longthorpe Tower is a hidden jewel. It is an outstanding example of a fortified medieval manor house. In the words of English Heritage it possesses 'the finest fourteenth-century domestic wall paintings in northern Europe, showing many secular and spiritual subjects, including *The Wheel of Life* and *The Nativity and King David*'. It is, quite simply, stunning.

---

*The quotation comes from an excellent booklet (obtainable in the Cathedral) by Paul Bush, *The Painted Ceiling of Peterborough Cathedral*, 2nd ed (2001). Published by Paul Bush, Simmondley House, Glossop SK13 6LS

Further Reading

Flag Fen

The archaeology of Flag Fen, Fengate and Northey is fully discussed in *The Flag Fen Basin: Archaeology and environment of a Fenland landscape* by Francis Pryor, English Heritage Archaeological Report (London, 2001). This detailed report includes the power station excavations and results from recent commercial work in the area. It is particularly notable for major papers on woodworking technology (by Maisie Taylor), metalwork (by the late David Coombs) and vegetation and environment (by Rob Scaife). This report also includes an overview of the palaeoenvironment (by Charles French), a reassessment of radiocarbon dates (by Alex Bayliss), many smaller reports and comprehensive references.

Earlier work at Flag Fen (much of it not discussed again in the Flag Fen Basin Report) has been published in: Pryor, F.M.M.; French, C.A.I. and Taylor, M. (1986), 'Flag Fen, Fengate Peterborough I: Discovery, Reconnaissance and Initial Excavation (1982-85)', Proceedings of the Prehistoric Society, vol 42, pp.1-24.

Fengate

The Fengate campaigns of 1971-'78 are comprehensively covered in four reports; the first is mainly devoted to a Neolithic 'house', middle Iron Age pits at Padholme Road and an early Iron Age settlement at Vicarage Farm: Francis Pryor, *Excavation at Fengate, Peterborough, England: the First Report*, Royal Ontario Museum Archaeology Monograph 3 (Toronto, 1974).

The second report is entirely given over to a Late Neolithic site on the Storey's Bar Way sub-site: Francis Pryor, *Excavation at Fengate, Peterborough, England: The Second Report*, Royal Ontario Museum Archaeology Monograph 5 (Toronto, 1978).

The third report considers the Bronze Age drove and enclosure system, with special reference to the Newark Road sub-site: Francis Pryor, *Excavation at Fengate, Peterborough, England: the Third Report*, Northamptonshire Archaeological Society Archaeological Monograph I/Royal Ontario Museum Archaeology Monograph 6 (Toronto and Leicester, 1980).

The fourth report covers the large Middle and Late Iron Age settlement at Cat's Water, a Neolithic multiple burial, also at Cat's Water and remaining Iron Age features at Vicarage Farm: Francis Pryor, *Excavation at Fengate, Peterborough, England: the Fourth Report*, Northamptonshire Archaeological Society Archaeological Monograph 2/Royal Ontario Museum Archaeological Monograph 7 (Toronto and Leicester, 1984).

Northey

The most recent source on Northey is chapter 5 of the Flag Fen Basin Report (see above).

Glossary

alluvium

A fine-grained, sticky clay which is deposited by rivers, usually in winter, during times of flood. Alluviation is the process whereby alluvium is laid down.

awl (or bradawl)

A small pointed implement, usually in metal, used to make holes, but without a drilling action.

Bronze Age

The period following the Neolithic, from *c*.2500-800/700 BC, which sees the adoption of metalworking in copper and bronze (an alloy mainly of copper, with tin, and sometimes lead too).

coppice

Certain trees and shrubs can be cut back at regular intervals to provide long, thin and straight poles or rods. If this is done at ground level it is termed coppicing, and the gnarled wood from which the shoots grow is known as a coppice 'stool' (see also **pollard**).

Cretaceous

The third and last age of reptiles (dinosaurs), 140-65 million years ago. The chalk hills of England date to this period (see also **Jurassic**).

dendrochronology

The study of tree-rings as a means of providing precise dates. Dendrochronologists can also provide important information on forest/woodland management and climate.

drove

A shortening of 'droveway', a road or track specifically intended for driving animals and their herdsmen or drovers. In the Fens droves from drier land into the seasonally available wet pastures were an important feature of the landscape.

henge

Derived from Stone*henge*. A class of Late Neolithic (*c*.3000-2500 BC) ceremonial sites involving one or more large circular ditches, sometimes enclosing a setting of posts or stones. They are only found in Britain and Ireland.

humify

To convert into humus, the organic component of the topsoil. In peat lands humification, which requires oxygen, follows swiftly upon drainage. It is a process highly detrimental to organic archaeological deposits.

Iron Age

(700/800 BC-AD43) The period following the Bronze Age which sees the widespread adoption of iron as the main tool- and weapon-making metal. Iron smelting requires sophisticated fire and furnace technology.

Jurassic

The great age of reptiles, 195-140 million years ago; in England blue Oxford Clay was laid down in its warm seas (see also **Cretaceous**).

La Tène

A small lake in Switzerland in which were found large numbers of Iron Age swords and other items, placed in the waters as offerings. The **typological** development of these items is used to provide the chronological framework for the later Iron Age of continental Europe, from *c*.450 BC until the Roman Conquest.

marine transgression

A period when the sea covered large areas of low-lying land. When the waters retreated we talk of a regression phase.

Mesolithic or Middle Stone Age. The period which follows the Upper Palaeolithic and the last Ice Age (about 10,000 years ago). People subsisted on hunting, gathering and fishing and made distinctive fish-spears and arrowheads from very small flakes of flint, known as microliths.

Neolithic or New Stone Age. The period of the first farmers (in Britain c.4300-2500 BC). It follows the Mesolithic and sees the widespread adoption of pottery and stone technologies that involved the use of grinding and polishing.

overburden

A general term to describe topsoil or other material that lies over (thereby concealing) archaeological deposits.

Palaeolithic or Old Stone Age. The earliest archaeological period (in Britain c.600,000 – 10,000 years ago). In Europe the Palaeolithic dates to the Ice Ages, when mankind survived by hunting and gathering wild foods.

palaeosol

An ancient soil. Palaeosols usually survive buried beneath burial mounds, ditch banks etc. In the Fens they can be found covering large areas of land, beneath later deposits of peat and **alluvium**.

palstave

The main axe type of the Middle Bronze Age. It consists of a flat piece of bronze with raised side-walls and a stop-ridge against which a split shaft is bound.

pollard

Certain trees, especially willows, grow long, straight shoots if they are cut back regularly. Pollards are trees cut back, usually above head height, to keep the young shoots clear of browsing animals (see also **coppice**).

radiocarbon dating

A dating method used for organic materials, such as wood, charcoal, or bone. All living things absorb mildly radioactive carbon which breaks down at a uniform rate upon death; this rate of decay can be measured to provide a date.

roddon or rodham

An extinct, silt-filled tidal creek bed. Most are of prehistoric age and traverse large tracts of Fenland. They are best seen in peaty soils where the white of the roddon silts contrasts strongly with the dark peats.

sock a local traditional Fenland term for the ground water-table. 'Sock wells' penetrate to the sock, and are usually no more than 2m (6ft) deep.

subsoil

The material immediately below the topsoil, from which it is partly composed. The nature of the subsoil dictates the type of topsoil that will form on it; thus a clay subsoil gives rise to a heavy topsoil.

turbaries

Land set-aside for peat-cutting, usually for fuel.

typology

An archaeological system that arranges the chronological development of any given site or artefact into a progression of stages. Thus the typological development of Bronze Age axes starts with simple flat axes, progresses to flanged axes, palstaves and culminates, in the Late Bronze Age, with socketed axes.

use-life

The period when a site or building was actually in use.

Index

Page numbers in **bold** refer to illustrations

Abbott, G.W. 43-4, 56, 97, 156, 166, 178
aerial photography **62**, 73-6, 167, 195
alluvium 19, 22, 32, 42, 88, 96, 116, 119, 128
Anglian Water (Authority/PLC) 26-7, 46, 51,
    1-2, 107-8
anthropological archaeology 59, 161
armlet, inlaid 139, 155, **colour plate 18**
Artis, E.T. 42-3
Assendelft 103, 116
Avebury 55, 77, 95
Axes 59, 66, 68, 72, 81, 86-7, 103-4, 107, 111,
    120, 122, 137, **148-150**, 151, 154-5

barrows 15, 44, 57, 75, 89-91, 95-7, 155
Bedford Rivers/Levels 22, 57
'bog oaks' 24-**25**, 103
bogs, as habitats 19-20, 138
bones, animal 69, 83, 88, 116, 125, **134**, 140, 172
bones, human 66, **67-68**, 70, 114, 140, **173**, **174**
borehole survey 54, 110, 122, **123**, 157
Borough Fen, Peterborough **20**, 90
Boudica 175
Boundaries **colour plate 10**, **32**, 36, 59-60, 73,
    82-4, 96
Bradley, Prof. R.J 73, 155, 159
Bradley Fen **colour plate 30**, 152, 177
British Museum, The 9, 69. 82. 112, 118, 137,
    166, 167
Bronze Age
    barrows 15, 44, 89-91, 95, 97, 155
    burial (without a barrow) **colour plate 10**
    fields 11, 73, 84, 166

houses **colour plates 7-9**, 85-88
landscape 72ff
life and death in 91-8
metalwork 52, 55, 82, 98,125,133ff, **135-6**,
    137-40, 153-64, **colour plates 14-17, 28**
brooches **colour plate 17**, 98, 125, 139, 153,
    158, 160

Caergwrle bowl 139
Cambridge 20, 57, 137
Candidus, Hugh 12, 41
carpentry **105**, 120, 151, 162
Cat's Water sub-site
    Bronze Age 37, 128
    Iron Age **colour plate 29**, **31-2**, 166ff
    Neolithic 69ff
    Roman 175
Cat's Water, drain 36, 41, 54, 68
Clare, John 43
'co-axial' fields 84
Coombs, Dr D.G. 52, 137, 139, 180
Coppice 118, 151, 181
Craddock, Dr P. 82, 167
crannogs 116
Cranstone, 66
cremation 78, 97, 174
Cretaceous period 19
cropmarks 30ff, **31-2**, 61 74, 83, 167
Crowther, David 106
Crucible 139
Cunliffe, Prof. B.W. 43
Current Archaeology 45

daggers **colour plate 15**, 125, 133, 138-9

Darby, Prof. H.C. 22

Darrah, Richard 103

Dartmoor Reaves 84

daub 119, 140, 162, 168

dendrochronology (see also tree-ring dating) 138

Denmark 59, 72

Denver 102, 175

Dog-in-a-Doublet sluice 42, 102

dog burials **134,** 140

Dove, Simon 137

dredging 24

droveways **colour plates 5-7,** 9, 11, 40, **62, 75,**
80-1, 82ff, 90-1, 161, 167, 170-1, 178

Durobrivae 40, 102, 175

'Dyke Survey' 30, 33, 46, 99, 101

dykes 14, 22, 24-6, 46, 53, 90, 99-102, 104-109,
110, 111, **114,** 116, 122-4, 157

earth moving 34, **35,** 63, 74, 76, 81, 135

Edgren, Dr Bengt 88

English Heritage 17, 28, 46, 51-3, 60, 69, 73, 89,
99, 109, 113, 123, 126

erosion see also 'peat shrinkage' 23

excarnation 97, 174

excavation techniques 33-40

experimental archaeology 86, 89, 103, 161-2,
163, 164

Eye, Cambs. 43, 100, 101

farming, arrival of 57-61

Fell, C.I. 43

Fen Causeway, the 31, **32,** 102, 175

Fen Clay 16-17, 19

'Fen Tigers' 22

Fengate **colour plates 3, 5, 6, 10, 29, 30,**
passim 30-99, 160-77

Fengate sub-sites explained 36

Fengate Ware 9

Fenland Archaeological Trust 49, 51

Fenland Project 89, 135

fens, as habitats 19-20

the Fens 12-29

abuse of 90

Bronze Age 17, 89-90

drainage 21-5

formation 17-18

map of **10**

fishing 22, 61, 74, 172

Flag Fen

artificial lake 26, 27-8, 29

ceremonial and ritual 153-9

defined 9

discovery 46

display and education 46-53

funding 46

the platform 120-22

the post alignment 140-153

flag iris 29

Fleming, A. 84

flints

Bronze Age 68, 76

Neolithic 64, 66, 96

Floors 116

Fourth Drove sub-site 83, 85, 88

Fox, Sir C. 57

French, Dr C.A.I. 100, 106-7, 111, 117, 170

fuel 20, 24

Green, John 185

Grimes, Prof. W.F. 34, 45-6

Grooved Ware **77,** 78-9

Gurney, David 106

Haddenham, Cambs. 89-90

Hall, D.N. 21-2, 60, 89

Hawker Siddeley Power Engineering Ltd 128

Hawkes, C.F.C. 43

Heathrow 34, 45

helmets 139

Helpston 43

Henges 15, 77, 94-7

Hereward the Wake 40

Holland 24, 46, 60, 103, 116

Holme-next-the-Sea 45

Holme Fen **23,** 24-5

Huntingdon 19

Independent, The 134
Iron Age
    burials **173-4**
    farming 11, 161, 171
    metalwork **colour plates 16-7**, 158-9

Jurassic period 19, 50

Kinnes, Dr I.A. 69

landscape 14-24, 40-2, 72-4, 175-7
Langdale 66, 68, 96
Leeds, E.T. 43-4
Leiden University 113
Little Butser 86, 162
loom weights 74
Louwe-Kooijmans, Prof. L.P. 113
lustre, on flints 66

Mahany, C. 45, 61
March, Cambs. 102, 175
marine regressions and transgressions 18-0, 21
Marshland 16-9, 21
Maxey, Cambs. 46, 95-6
Medeshamstede 40
Mesolithic 57, 59, 60-1, 70
metal-detectors 34, 133-9, 158
molluscan analysis 100-1, 170
Montagu, Lord 26
Morton, Prior 21
Mustdyke, the 46, 49-50, 53-4, 102, 104, **108**,
    109, **111, 113**, 114, 122-3, **130**, 157

Nene, River 9, 102
Nene Valley 40-1, 160
Nene Valley Research Committee 44-5
Neolithic
    discussed in general 58-61
    'house' 63-6
    multiple burial 66-9
    ring-ditch **75**, 78-9
Neve, Janet 131
Newark Road sub-site 79, 83, 85, 88

Norfolk Broads 20
North Sea 17-22, 58-9, 60
Northey **colour plate 3**, 9-10, **11**, 13, 36, 50,
    84, 102, **113**, 130, 140, 151-3, 175, 177
nucleated settlement 11, 92, 159, 166

'open area' excavation 33-4, 39, 88, 132
opium poppy 172
ornaments 135-9, 153-5, 157
Ouse, River 19, 22, 91

Padholme Road sub-site 63-8
palaeosols 101
peat or 'Black' Fen 19-21
'peat shrinkage' **23**, 118-9
perimeter revetment 120-3
Peterborough
    archaeological research in 42-6
    City 40
    Museum 67-8, 165, 175
    New Town 44-5, 53
    styles of pottery 44
    R.C.H.M. report 44
phosphate analysis 52-3, 167-8
pins **colour plates 14, 17, 28**, 98, 134, 137-9,
    160
pits 13, 30, 56, 61, 63, **65**, 69, 165, 166-7, 174
Pitt-Rivers, General 34
pollard 24, 118
pottery
    Bronze Age **colour plate 14**, 43, 111, **112**,
        115, 125, 141
    Iron Age 44, **48**, 162, 164-6
    Neolithic 43-4, 64, 66, 69, 76, **77**
    Roman 11, 40, 167
power station sub-site 36, 39, 42, 88, 96, 129, 140
Preservation Hall **colour plates 1-2**, 52, 120
Private Eye 109
public archaeology 46-53

quarry pits 44, **76**, 78

radial split see woodworking

radiocarbon dating 25, 41, 55, 58, 73, 79, 112, 128, 150

rapiers **colour plate 15**, 138, 158

razors **colour plate 17**, 98

religion see ritual

Reynolds, Dr P. 86, 162

ring-ditch **32**, 75, **76**, 77-8, 95

rings 138-9, 153

ritual, discussed 69-70, 91-5, 153-9

'ritual landscapes' 9, 95-6

Rivenhall 70

roddons or rodhams 18-19, 32, **33**

Royal Commission on Historic Monuments 44-5, 74

Royal Ontario Museum 45, 82

salt 19, 21, 41, 42, 84, 152

Sayers, Dorothy 16-7

Scabbard **colour plates 15, 28, 126**, 127, **135**, 138, 153, 156, 160

scoop, willow 120

'Seahenge' 45

seasonal movement see transhumance

sedge 14, 20, 24, 122, 162, 170

Selkirk, A. 45

'settlement drift' 166

shale bracelet **colour plates 14, 18**, 11, 118, 125, 139-41, 153, 155

shears **colour plate 16**, 134, 139, 160

sheep, Soay 88, **92**, 94

shields **135**, 138-9

sill-plate 119

Site 11 61-3

Smith, Dr I. 43

Smith, Prof. R.A. 43

'sock' or water table **colour plate 4**, 56, 77, **170**

soil science 100-1

micromorphology 101

Somerset 26, 75, 89, 106, 107, 129, 132

spears **colour plates 15, 28**, 59, **135**, 138, 140, 153-4

Spencer, John 87

Sphagnum moss 20

Splitting see woodworking

sprinkler system **colour plate 1**

St Joseph, Prof. J.K. 44

steam pumps 24

Storey's Bar Way sub-site 75-9

Sweden 88, 117

Sweet Track, Somerset 26

swords **colour plates 14, 15, 28**, p. **38**, 39, 98, **126**, 127, **133**, 134, **135**, 138-40, 153, 155-6, 158, 160

sword, miniature **colour plate 15**, 138, 140

tangential split (see also woodworking) **colour plates 11, 26**, 103-4, 106, 119, 141

Taylor, C.C. 44, 74, 81

Taylor, Maisie **colour plate 30**, 103, 107, 108, 119, 120, 132, 150, 151, 176

thatch and thatching 12, 20, 24, 41, 86-8, **165**, 168, 169

timber see woodworking

Time Team 37, **38**, 150

tin **colour plate 17**, 138-9

tool-marks 107, 125

trackways **colour plate 30**, 26, 46, 52, 74-5, 79, 81, 83-4, 106-7, 129, 151

transhumance 60

tree-ring dating 25, 131-3, 141, 153, 157

turbaries 22

turf roofing **colour plate 8**, 53, **81**, 87-8, 168-9

Tushingham, Dr A.D. 45

'uncertainty principle' 115

Vermuyden, C. 22

Vicarage Farm sub-site 42, 67-9, 166, 171

Wainwright, Dr G.J. 109, 111, 123

Washland 22

weapons 38, 138, 153-5, 157-8

Welland valley 46, 83, 91, 95-6, 109

wells see 'sock'

Wessex 55-6, 77, 95, 97-8

wheels, metal **colour plate 17**

wheel, wooden **colour plate 27**, 153

Whittlesey Mere 20, 23, 25

Wicken Fen 20

Wilburton tradition 138-40

Wild, Dr J.P. 45

windmills 16, 24

Wisbech 16-7, 21, 40, 102, 107

woodworking **colour plate 26**, 103-4, 147-51

If you are interested in purchasing other books published by Tempus,
or in case you have difficulty finding any Tempus books in your local bookshop,
you can also place orders directly through our website

www.tempus-publishing.com